THE ALLIANCED ENTERPRISE

Global Strategies for Corporate Collaboration

THE ALLIANCED ENTERPRISE

Global Strategies for Corporate Collaboration

Editors

Ard-Pieter de Man

CEO, Centre for Global Corporate Positioning (CGCP)
The Netherlands

Geert Duysters

Scientific Director, Eindhoven Centre for Innovation Studies (ECIS)
The Netherlands

Ash Vasudevan

Managing Director, CommerceNet Investment Initiatives
USA

centre for global corporate positioning

Imperial College Press

Published by

Imperial College Press
57 Shelton Street
Covent Garden
London WC2H 9HE

Distributed by

World Scientific Publishing Co. Pte. Ltd.
P O Box 128, Farrer Road, Singapore 912805
USA office: Suite 1B, 1060 Main Street, River Edge, NJ 07661
UK office: 57 Shelton Street, Covent Garden, London WC2H 9HE

British Library Cataloguing-in-Publication Data
A catalogue record for this book is available from the British Library.

ISBN   1-86094-290-3

Printed in Singapore by Mainland Press

BK Title

Foreword

autha p vii

There is no doubt that strategic alliances are among the most important trends in business today. "Strategic alliances are hot," says Matthew Schifrin, Editor, Forbes.com's Best of the Web Magazine in a recent issue. "This may be the most powerful trend that has swept American business in a century." According to recent studies, over 26% of the average Fortune 500 company's revenues are now derived from alliances and this figure is expected to reach 35% in the next several years.

Increasingly, firms recognize that alliances are a "Must Have Core Competency" if they are to compete effectively in today's rapidly changing, hyper-competitive, global marketplace with its rapid pace of technological change, exploding consumer choice and increased uncertainty. In fact, the convergence of the Internet and alliances has driven the emergence of a new business model, "The Networked Enterprise", creating constellations of aligned firms as the basic competitive unit, transforming the very nature of the firm.

Companies have found alliances a powerful tool for decreasing technological and market risk, speeding new products to market, leapfrogging the competition in the creation of new markets and driving growth and profits. Moreover, recent research suggests that shareholder value is significantly enhanced by alliance activity. Share prices tend to react favorably to announcements of alliances, even more so than to announcements of mergers and acquisitions and companies with a dedicated alliance function and competency have found an even more dramatic impact on stock prices from alliance announcements than their peers.

Alliances have proven to be a ubiquitous tool for driving growth, educing costs and risks and improving the delivery of integrated solutions to customers. Yet, alliances pose challenges to management as well. They require a different approach from the more traditional "Command and Control" management model. They can be difficult to create and manage effectively. They require dedicated resources and adoption of Alliance Best Practices to maximize their effectiveness. However, by creating dedicated alliance programs and adopting Alliance Best Practices, studies have shown that firms can improve their alliance success rates dramatically, some studies suggesting that they can reach over 75%.

The Association of Strategic Alliance Professionals (A.S.A.P.) was created to support the professional development of alliance managers and executives, to advance the state-of-the-art of alliance formation and management and to provide a central forum for sharing alliance best practices, resources and opportunities to help companies improve their alliance management capabilities. A.S.A.P. is constantly striving to meet this goal by organizing conferences, publishing best practice books, supporting research and acting as a central forum and resource for alliance professionals. This book is another example of this kind of activity.

This book provides an overview of the most relevant issues in alliance management today. Some of the leading experts involved in writing this book, many of them involved in A.S.A.P., express the latest in alliance thinking. The theme running through this book, that firms will have to learn how to manage a large number of alliances effectively, is one that will resonate with all alliance managers. In the contacts A.S.A.P. has with hundreds of alliance professionals each year, there is one thing that stands out, i.e. as the number of alliances grows, there is a corresponding increased need for new management tools, alliance models and best practices. This book addresses these issues and therefore it is a valuable and timely contribution to the field of alliance management.

The articles in this book cover a range of important topics alliance managers are struggling with. How can alliances be used in an Internet setting? How to design alliance networks? Which alliance skills and capabilities are required? Real-life cases from alliance-intensive firms show how these firms have answered these questions. This combination of leading-edge ideas and practical cases will make this book an important contribution to the emerging body of best practices in alliance formation and management and a valuable and enjoyable resource for alliance professionals.

I am confident that the lines laid down in this book will continue to remain relevant, simply because the Alliance Enterprise is the business organizational form of the future. Alliance managers experience this everyday.

William T. Lundberg,
Founding President and Executive Director,
Association of Strategic Alliance Professionals (A.S.A.P.)

Contents

Bk Title : **Introduction**

eds

NIA

Throughout the business world today, the competitive landscape is rapidly changing. Innovation, new value-creating propositions, blurring industry boundaries, and intensifying competition on a global scale are all driving businesses to form new connections and alliances at an unprecedented rate. The digital revolution that has engulfed us and profoundly changed our lives in unimaginable ways has been greatly facilitated by this alliance revolution that has fundamentally changed the way companies acquire resources, build capabilities, develop core competencies, and seek ways to create, build and sustain their competitive advantage. The alliance revolution that is presently sweeping the global economic landscape involves companies creating "value webs" that integrate specialized resources, specialized capabilities and specialized competencies, to develop new rules, new ideas, new markets, and offer fundamentally new value propositions. These connections have led to the emergence of the network economy, profoundly impacting businesses in the process. If anything, success in the new millennium will be greatly dependent on your firm's ability to formulate and implement at all levels strategies for developing and leveraging a wide array of alliances.

We now live in an economic environment that is non-linear, discontinuous, and changing at an extraordinary rate. In one industry after another, we are seeing the entry of new firms from unusual and hitherto unexpected directions, bringing in new thinking, new technologies, new attitudes, new market-shaping concepts, and most importantly radically new price/performance capabilities for products and services. Now more than ever, firms are faced with the critical and daunting challenge of maintaining the cutting edge of their core competencies while simultaneously striving to maintain the feverish pace at which they must develop and introduce a slew of new products and services. However, today's new product and service innovations are typically an amalgamation of several distinct and complex technological capabilities drawn from multiple industries and serving multiple needs of a single consumer. Take the case of the new smart card that is expected to perform diverse functions integrating competencies from multiple industries by being a credit card, debit card, ATM card, library card, phone card, frequent flier mileage tracker, and car key, as well as enabling its owner to buy a latte from a coffee house, a hot dog from a station vendor, beer at the baseball park, feed a parking meter and pay a toll. No single firm, regardless of the size, could singe-handedly produce such a product anymore. The current economic environment demands the melding together of complex, heterogeneous resources and capabilities of organizations that are usually dissimilar in culture, size, industry, and often country of origin, as a basis for simultaneously creating and destroying wealth. That collaboration can be rewarding is no longer a mystery that needs perennial validation. In fact, Booz, Allen and Hamilton's study on alliances states that nearly 35% of the revenues of the top 1000 firms is expected to come from alliances. Building an alliance network frequently provides the firm with a portfolio of options to exercise in the face of rapid change at a relatively low cost. Now, alliances not only serve as windows of opportunities to be exploited, but also provide the means to neutralize threats. Clearly, now more than ever, alliances among firms are profoundly changing the conventional wisdom of going it alone, and their virtual explosion is a testament to their growing importance.

Co-operation today has emerged as a prerequisite to effective competition. Aiming to establish a dominant position in the corporate and consumer wireless communication markets, an alliance between Microsoft and British Telecom on the one hand is competing against an alliance between Cisco and Motorola on the other. Also, computer giant IBM recently teamed up with electronics giant Sony, to develop competing standards for online music distribution, standards that are being concurrently developed by a network of Microsoft allies and another network of AT&T allies. Competition has now shifted from the conventional "Me against you" to "Us against them." Alliances are no longer a second-order condition of competition, but are rapidly emerging as the first order condition. So much so that "Cooperate or Perish" is no longer an idle mantra. In fact, the slogan promoted by Cable & Wireless: "The firm is dead — long live the federation," is emblematic of the trend towards "competition through cooperation."

This volume can be seen as an effort to share best practices in the rapidly evolving field of alliance management. We invited some well-known thought leaders on alliance management to participate in our endeavor to gain a deeper understanding of the underlying factors influencing the alliance life cycle. Without specific directions we asked them to write a chapter on their assessment of the most important aspects of alliance management. In their contributions, they stress those issues that they feel are germane and most critical to surviving the network economy. These contributions, therefore, reflect their view on the most important challenges we are facing in the field of alliance management.

The result of this approach is that we are able to present a mix of articles. In this volume different approaches can be found: theoretical and empirical, descriptive and normative, reflective and active ("how to"). Despite this diversity, somewhat to our surprise one red line emerged, which we may summarize as embeddedness. Apparently all authors agree on the idea that the alliance era is changing into a network era, in which firms are embedded in a large number of multilateral alliances. Moreover, the authors implicitly point out that networks are more than just a complicated form of bilateral alliances. Almost all contributions to this book describe specific laws, tools, mindsets and design criteria for networks. This suggests that networks require a type of management distinct from the management of bilateral alliances. Networks are more than the sum of alliances: they ask for new capabilities in managing the embedded firm. Clearly, the state of the art in research and practice has moved beyond alliance management towards management of networks.

The first chapter in this book, by Ash Vasudevan and Geert Duysters, provides a network perspective on alliances. It discusses the emergence of "value webs" that integrate specialized resources, specialized capabilities and specialized competencies, to develop new rules, new ideas, new markets, and offer fundamentally new value propositions. These complex inter-organizational networks offer firms the ability to access, leverage and integrate diverse knowledge streams. However, managing these networks requires a new approach to alliance management. In this chapter the authors discuss new portfolio management tools as well as other means to increase the alliance capabilities of companies. A case in point is the description of the impact of Philip's acquisition of VLSI on the strategic position of Philips in the global alliance network.

A new approach to alliance management is in particular required for so-called E-alliances is argued in the second chapter by John Bell. He argues that E-alliances have some characteristics which differentiate them from regular strategic alliances. To become a successful E-alliance player, firms should build up new alliance capabilities which suit the demands posed in The New Economy. Most of the alliance capabilities required in The Old Economy are likely to prevail, albeit they must be transformed to better meet the need for speed.

Managerial imperatives for competing in alliance constellations are the theme of the third chapter, contributed by Benjamin Gomes-Casseres and James Bamford. The authors argue that an increasing number of firms tend to move away from one-to-one competition towards so-called "group-based" competition in which companies compete in constellations — groups of firms linked together through alliances. Nowadays, effective constellation strategies seem to have become essential to competitive advantage in many industries. The success of constellations seems to depend on four basic choices: constellation size, membership mix, internal rivalry and collective governance. The authors describe how firms can successfully design constellations based on those choices.

This change towards networks has important consequences for management. Daisy Geurts and Han van der Zee argue this in Chapter 4.

Based on case research the authors show that alliance management differs from network management in a number of respects. Among these are planning, evaluation and the locus of management responsibility. These ideas are illustrated by lively case studies from two well-known new economy partnerships: the KPMG–Cisco alliance and the WAP Forum network.

In line with the previous chapter, Carlos García-Pont argues in Chapter 5 that firms are "embedded" in a network of cooperative agreements that influence the available options for each one of the firms in the network. García-Pont discusses three laws of alliance formation: 1) First mover advantage and imitation shape strategic blocks, 2) membership of a strategic block is likely to be exclusive, 3) alliance networks are a response to an imperfect market for strategic capabilities. These laws change our conception of the firm, as a distinct entity operating in one value chain. Instead, firms are part of many value chains, none of which is under their complete control. Moreover, firms will participate in different alliance groupings depending on the business or the activity it has at hand.

In Chapter 6, Larraine Segil addresses the important issue of preemptive alliances. The main motive behind a preemptive alliance is for one or more of the partners to preempt a competitor. Although these kinds of alliances have been in use for decades, their importance has increased tremendously in today's e-economy. It has become a fine art in which the most experienced players are rewarded handsomely. Segil shows that more than 58% of firms are involved in grabber-type situations and therefore preemption should be part of every company's portfolio of alliance methodologies.

The next chapters take a closer look at the internal side of the embedded firm. In Chapter 7 Ard-Pieter de Man views alliance capability as a source of competitive advantage and shows what management tools firms need to implement in order to raise the success rate of their alliances. When firms are capable of managing alliances, he argues, firms can create a distinctive position vis-à-vis competitors. Organizing for alliances may also have spectacular effects on alliance success rates.

In Chapter 8 Van Aken critically describes the efforts of multinational enterprises (MNEs) that are anxiously trying to use alliances as vehicles to increase their flexibility. In this chapter, two approaches to alliance management are discussed: the design approach and the learning approach. The design approach invests more effort in analysis of context, strategy and the set-up of the collaboration, whereas the learning approach has a more evolutionary character in which networks of relations develop on the basis of social interactions. For MNEs the latter approach poses quite some challenges. The basic lesson is that MNEs need to adapt their organization structure if they are to be effective in managing alliances and networks.

Following this line of thought, Robert Porter Lynch, argues that there are four critical alliance management skills that lay the foundation for a company to efficaciously manage and extract value from its strategic alliances. These skills are associated with excellence in managing differences, managing breakthroughs, managing speed of decision making and skills in managing transformation.

Chapter 10, authored by Bonnie Beerkens and Charmianne Lemmens, analyzes the various types of alliances that firms have at their disposal when dealing with the turbulence of high technology sectors. They argue that firms that have created the right mix of alliance types in their alliance portfolio will be better able to meet the challenges of a high tech business environment. Taking on a social network perspective on alliances, the authors distinguish among types of relationships and managerial alliance types. The aim of this chapter is to provide management with a better view on their alliance portfolio.

The next two chapters take an internal company perspective on alliances. Chapter 11 starts with an insider's view on how Philips Electronics deals with the issue of alliances. Guy Kerpen, one of Philips senior alliance managers provides a top management perspective on Philips' use of corporate alliances. Kerpen shares the best practices of Philips with the reader. Philips has recently implemented a number of management tools: new alliance management functions have been created, a website was developed and an alliance database installed. Two cases (3M and Microsoft) are used to illustrate the effectiveness of the Philips approach towards alliances.

Pieter Bouw, former CEO of KLM, provides another insiders' perspective in Chapter 12. One of the first CEOs to realize the importance of alliances for airlines, Bouw shares his experience with alliances in the airline industry. The chapter drafts a CEO's agenda for alliance management. From this chapter, four major consecutive phases of alliance management can be derived: i.e. establishing the reasons for partnering; getting to know your partner; concluding the alliance; managing implementation. Bouw provides best practices by sharing his experiences as a CEO when dealing with one of the most successful alliances in airline history (KLM–Northwest).

We conclude this volume with a broad perspective on alliances. Arvind Parkhe addresses the important issue of cooperation — specifically raising the question "does a true culture of cooperation exist?" Parkhe foresees a number of changes in how firms deal with alliances; i.e. companies will become more alliance-sophisticated, they will invest more resources in alliances, executive staffing will be powerfully affected and there will be growing appreciation of the soft aspects of collaboration. According to him, there are still some hurdles that impede companies from building a true culture of cooperation. This chapter shows that firms still have a long way to go, not only in adapting their organization structures, but even more fundamentally in adapting their mindset as well.

Returning to the theme of embeddedness, these chapters give a *tour d'horizon* of how being embedded in a network affects firms. Clearly, alliance management has come a long way. The cases in this book show the incredible amount and variety of alliance management approaches which have been developed over the last years. Looking forward into the future, the conclusion seems to be warranted that we are not there yet. Networks bring new challenges and threats. Importantly, these are not only of an instrumental nature, but of a psychological nature as well. Only when "hard" management tools are combined with "soft" aspects like creating alliance cultures, are firms ready to face their future of embeddedness.

Chapter 1

The Changing Face of Alliance Management: Managerial Imperatives for the Network Economy

(selected countries)

Ash Vasudevan, Geert Duysters, Ad van den Oord
and Svenn Bakkes

L24
L14

As the total number of alliances has increased over the years, so have the average number of alliances formed by individual firms. In industry after industry, we have seen a dramatic increase in the number of alliances formed by individual companies. Companies now find themselves embedded in a web of alliances integrating a wide variety of resources and capabilities. However, while alliances themselves have evolved from the alliance dyads of the post-industrial age to alliance networks in the digital age, managerial thinking has not concomitantly evolved to adapt to their changing forms. An incontestable truth in the network economy is that the strategic value of alliances can only be fully exploited if attention is paid to the overall network in which a firm is embedded. Below we delineate crucial characteristics of networks and offer some prescriptive concepts and tools that corporations will need to extract value from them.

Understanding Networks

As elucidated earlier, the increase in the number of alliances has led to the emergence of complex inter-organizational networks in which firms

9

are linked to each other either directly or indirectly. Embedded in the networks are relationships involving varying degrees of commitment and intent; relationships that could include the following:

- the means to acquire and leverage capabilities for value-creation upstream and downstream,
- the means for accessing and combining knowledge of different partners to develop cutting-edge solutions,
- the means to increase differentiation of products and services, and
- the means to improve competitive positions in present markets, and to take options in the future.

In such an environment, characterized by a mix of co-operation and competition, it is not sufficient to manage alliances on an individual, ad-hoc basis. Managing alliance networks involves gaining an overall appreciation of their critical characteristics such as the control points in the networks, the roles of the different actors, the structure of relations among different actors, the location of different actors in the network, the benefits and costs associated with different network positions, and the location of different strategic blocks within the network. It is also important to structure and manage them on a dynamic basis as the characteristics of networks evolve with time. Another critical issue to consider is the consequence of actions deployed by any one company within the network on the network's shape and form. An action could either be strategic or tactical in nature. A strategic action is devised to improve the organization's long-term competitive position and typically involves significant, irreversible commitments such as long-term alliances involving significant financial and non-financial commitment, or an acquisition. A tactical action does not involve irreversible commitments but is devised to improve the current or near-term competitive position and consequently is easy to implement — for example, a price cut.

To illustrate this, let us look at a network maps (Figures 2 to 5) that shows the evolution of strategic technology alliance networks in the Application Specific Integrated Circuits (ASICs) industry from 1976 to 1996. From 1976–982, the network map displays no identifiable clusters. The number of alliances formed is also limited.

As we can see, the overall network structure of the industry has changed with time, from being sparse with no identifiable clusters in the early periods (see Figure 2) to dense clearly identifiable clusters in the latter period (see Figure 4). Both the number of alliances and the number of firms forming alliances have increased from 136 to 397 and 100 to 290 respectively. Concomitant with the evolution of the industry, we can see the emergence of strategic blocks between 1983–1989. A strategic block is a sub-network of firms that are more densely tied to each other than the rest of the members in the network. We can observe two such blocks, one involving a cluster of mainly North

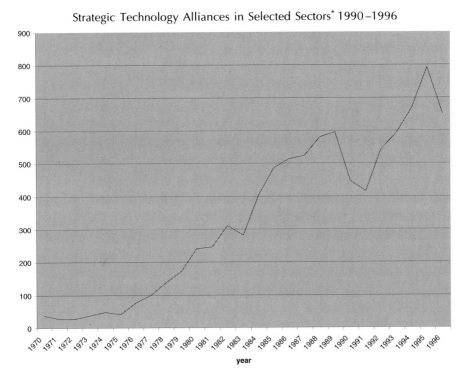

Strategic Technology Alliances in Selected Sectors* 1990–1996

Source: MERIT-CATI

Figure 1. Number of newly established strategic technology alliances, worldwide 1970–1996.

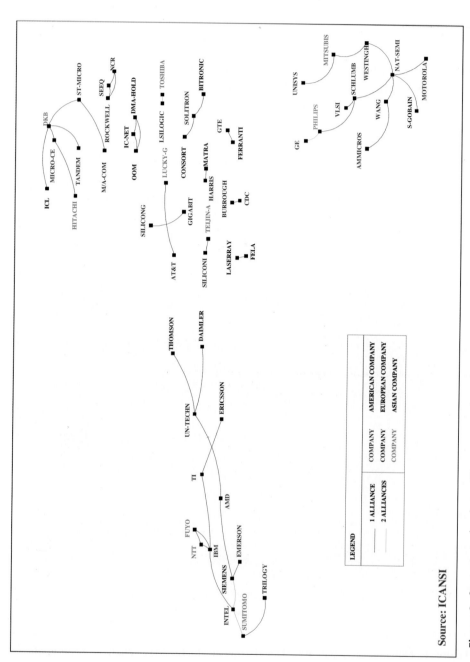

Figure 2. Strategic technology alliance network ASICS (Application Specific Integrated Circuits) industry 1976–1982.

Source: **ICANSI**

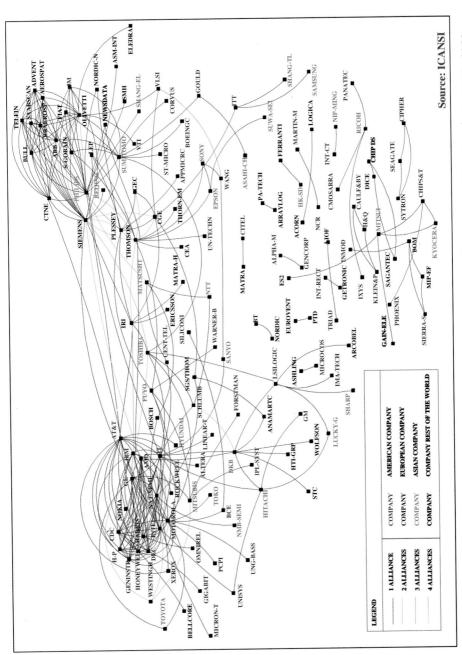

Figure 3. Strategic technology alliance network ASICS (Application Specific Integrated Circus) industry 1983–1989.

Source: ICANSI

American firms (like Rockwell, Motorola, Hewlett Packard, IBM) and another involving a cluster of mainly European firms (including Siemens, Bull, Olivetti, Fiat). You can easily see that the North American cluster is denser than the European Cluster. Both the US and European blocks emerged in response to fears of losing competitive advantage, and both received government support. The US initiative was called SEMATECH (the Semiconductor Manufacturing Technology Project) and involved companies from a variety of industries. These included AMD, AT&T, DEC, Harris Corporation, HP, Intel, IBM, LSI Logic, Micron Technology Inc., Motorola, National Semiconductor Corporation, NCR, Rockwell International, and Texas Instruments. On the other hand, the European block was called JESSI (Joint European Submicron Silicon Initiative) and was led by Philips, Siemens and SGS-Thomson. So, what drives the emergence of such blocks? Typically, they are based on a commonality of interest, be it technology, markets, country, strategies, or core competencies.

From 1990–1996, we can see the disaggregation of the American Block, and the emergence of an Asian Block around among others Sony, Fujitsu, Matsushita (see Figure 4). This is consistent with the existing body of knowledge that has documented the emergence of Asian clusters as an industry evolves. However, both blocks are not as dense as those that emerged in Europe and the USA between 1983–1986 are. Now, consider again the network map in Figure 4. We can see that Philips (in the bottom right corner), has its own network of European firms and, by the virtue of its relationship with VLSI, a North American firm based in the Silicon valley, it also has access to a cluster of North American firms. Recently (May 1999), Philips acquired VLSI for approximately $1.04 billion. In addition to providing Philips with a better foothold and access to the US market, this acquisition is expected to play a crucial role for Philips as it expands into fast-growing markets such as mobile communications. In Figure 5, we can observe how the network map changed as a consequence of this strategic action (see Figure 6 for details). Based on its acquisition, the North American cluster surrounding VLSI is now positioned more closely to the European cluster surrounding Philips.

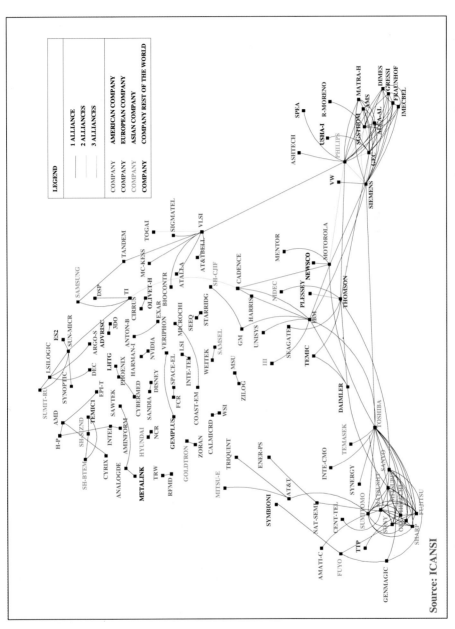

Figure 4. Strategic technology alliance network ASICS (Application Specific Integrated Circuits) industry 1990–1996.

Source: ICANSI

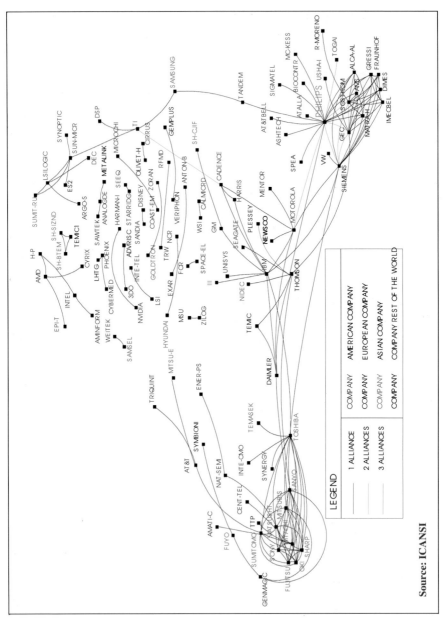

Figure 5. Strategic technology alliance network ASICS (Application Specific Integrated Circuits) industry 1990–1996 after Philips' aquistion of VLSI on May 1999.

Source: ICANSI

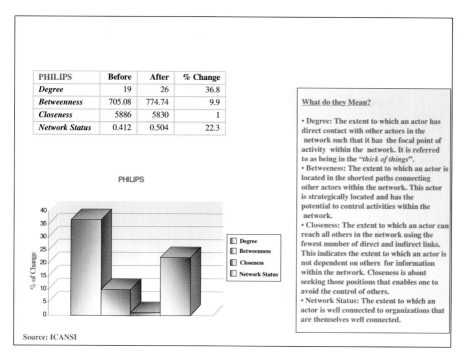

Figure 6. The changing role and position of Philips in the ASICS network: Before and after its acquisition of VLSI.

Also, Philips now has more alliances with other organizations than any other firm embedded in the network. This makes them more centrally located, thereby providing them with greater access to the networks' resources than anybody else.

Indeed, this acquisition now makes Philips not only the most connected, in terms of the number of firms linked to it, but also the best connected, in terms of the nature of those links (see Figure 6). What is also interesting to observe is the impact of this acquisition on some other key players within the network? How did the acquisition impact some other key players in the network (see Figure 7)? As one can observe, it has had a negative impact on Toshiba, Siemens, and IBM making them less influential in the ASICs network. Some lessons can be learned from the above discussion:

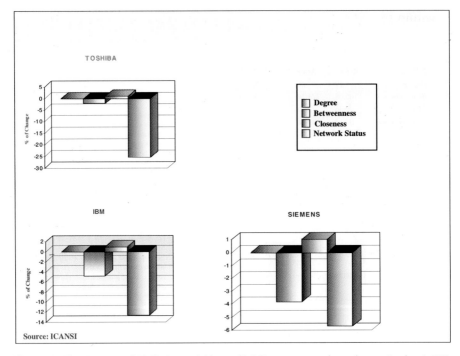

Figure 7. The impact of Philip's aquisition of VLSI on some other players in the ASIC's network.

1. A network's design or shape changes with time, thereby impacting on the roles and positions of different actors.
2. Over time there may be changes to the scarce positions from which you can control the critical and valuable aspects of the networks, such as information, finance, ideas, innovations.
3. The overall shape of the network, and the relations and positions defining the actors embedded in it are vulnerable to both endogenous events — for example, actions initiated by members within the network — and exogenous events — for example, new revolutionary technology emerging from outside the network.
4. Finally, the positions that offer maximum access to the sources of competitive advantage within the network may change with time. Managers must be able to constantly seek those scarce positions

within the network from which they can maximize their potential to contribute and exploit new value-seeking and value-creating propositions.

Now more than ever, managers cannot confine their time to simply managing their alliances on an individual basis. Managing them in isolation can lead to a loss of precious value-creating and value-capturing opportunities available through synergy. It is important to manage them both as networks of relationships involving your firm, and the overall network in which your firm is embedded. Managing in a network economy is about orchestrating actions to protect current wealth and seek new wealth. But how can this be accomplished? Our research at ICANSI has developed a few prescriptive guidelines for alliance managers in firms embedded in a web of relationships.

A Different View of Strategy: From Independence to Interdependence

"None are more hopelessly enslaved, than those who falsely believe they are free"

Goethe (1749–1832)

The underlying premise of the industrial economy, which emphasizes the importance of self-sufficiency and independence in managing a portfolio of products and businesses, is a notion that is dead in the digital economy (see Figure 8). Interdependence is at the heart of the network economy. Interdependence exists when one actor cannot entirely control all the conditions necessary to achieve a desirable outcome. Being dependent on the network for cutting-edge resources, capabilities and core competencies is now at the core of every company's competitive effort regardless of size, industry or country of origin. However, as a manager it is important to be cognizant of both the benefits that can be attained and the costs that can be incurred.

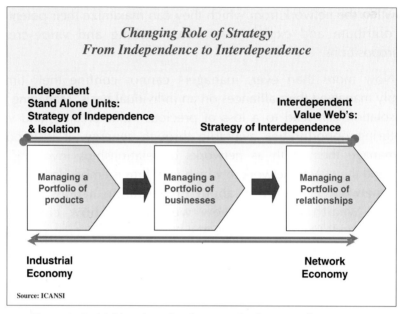

Figure 8. Rethinking the role of strategy in the network economy.

An individual firm's role in a network is also important. First you have to decide whether your firm is going to be either an integrator — combining various products into a complete offering for the client e.g. Toyota and Benetton, or a specialist — supplying a limited range of products to the network e.g. Intel and Goodyear. Having a clear position in a network makes a firm an attractive partner. Managers should therefore focus on the triple task of:

- constantly monitoring their role and position within the network,
- monitoring their advantage relative to others within the network, and
- devising strategies by which the entire block can be positioned effectively in relation to other competing blocks.

Managing Networks for Knowledge

In the network economy, companies can no longer maintain capabilities that are not world class, and increasingly must rely on richly connected relationships with specialists to create value webs. The ability to tackle diversity within networks is crucial and depends on the firm's ability to constantly seek new knowledge, leverage existing knowledge with other network partners, and manage the knowledge interface. This means seeking those positions in the network that enable firms to monitor and manage the flow of knowledge within the network. An equally important task is to be able to interpret the diversity of knowledge flowing within the network. ASM Lithography had an innovative solution to this problem. They appointed "cultural ambassadors" whose task it was to manage the flow of knowledge between specialists working in different scientific disciplines from different industries within its network. This assisted them greatly in improving the speed of their product development.

Accessing, leveraging and integrating diverse knowledge is critical if you want to be in the forefront of new business development. The current trend of conceiving solutions, instead of individual products services, in an attempt to offer "one stop shopping" to customers is a particularly illustrative. Solutions typically integrate diverse competencies spanning multiple industries. For instance an e-commerce solution today typically combines knowledge and skills from computers, systems integration, telecommunications, retailing, banking and credit card transaction services. An airlines solution includes a network of telephone companies, Internet shopping, hotels, restaurants, and car rentals toname a few. A solution in Biotech includes integrating diverse research fields such as carbohydrates, liposomes, gene therapy, combinatorial chemistry and genomics. Within the context of networks, the emphasis should be on managing alliances as a portfolio of competencies and on conceiving of new ways to integrate those competencies into new solutions. It is the combination of all the partners' competencies that provides the real benefit from a particular partnership. In this regard, some tools have been developed to manage networks, which will be discussed below.

Alliance Portfolio Management: What Is Your Alliance Bandwidth?

While bandwidth is the capacity to move information down a given channel, alliance bandwidth is a firm's capacity to form and manage different alliances, tap into the synergy between alliances, and successfully leverage those alliances for resources, capabilities and core competencies. Alliance bandwidth differs from company to company and from industry to industry. Often firms spend a lot of time aggressively recruiting partners but little time learning to managing them. Managing alliances as a portfolio can enable companies to determine their alliance bandwidth, constantly monitor their capability to manage alliances, and harness their value. It is important to constantly seek answers to the following questions:

- What are our current capabilities and what capabilities do we need to compete in current markets?
- What capabilities do we need to build to compete in future markets?
- How many of these capabilities can be built in-house and how many can be built through alliance networks?
- Which direction is our portfolio of relationships taking us?

Conducting such an analysis and building the right portfolio on an ongoing basis will enable a firm to effectively hedge against current and future trends, and to be on the right side of any technological and market discontinuities. Also, it is important to note that a firm can have various alliances with one partner. Making an inventory of these relationships and relating them to one another can indicate ways to avoid conflict or exploit possible synergies. Finally, an organization with a well-constructed portfolio of relationships is more attractive to other members in the networks because of the potential access that it can provide to resources and cutting-edge capabilities.

Establishing Partner Programs

Establishing partner programs is another critical tool in monitoring the network as a whole and in identifying its strengths and weaknesses.

Firms like FedEx, Oracle, Xerox, and HP have extensive partner programs, which help them maintain an overview of their large number of partners by classifying them, thus reducing the complexity of their networks. Another benefit of partner programs is that they enable firms to formulate rules with which to evaluate and monitor their network partners, based on their commitment to the network.

Creating a Database of Alliances

Given the rapid pace of alliance formation, companies frequently lose sight of the number of partners they actually have. Creating a central repository of all alliances is particularly useful in this context. A repository can enable firms to monitor their networks, register detailed knowledge about their network partners and share knowledge with others in the organization. HP, Federal Express, and Oracle are examples of companies that have created databases extensively documenting the intricacies of all their alliances. This has enabled them to expand their know-how and use it collaboratively to make better decisions on the why, what, how, when and with whom to form alliances.

Understanding the complexities of networks, and managing them efficiently enables companies both to compete effectively in their present markets and to continually be at the forefront of creating new ones. If managed well, alliances can be a source of new strategies, new ideas, new perspectives and new wealth-creation opportunities. At the corporate level, some of the benefits may include a superior ability to spot opportunities, attract valuable partners, and achieve a superior competitive position within the network and between networks. At the business level, the appreciation and efficacious management of networks can lead to consistently better price performance capabilities for a firm's products, and a superior ability to spot and respond to changing market dynamics. To do this, companies must acquire a capacity for creativity that taps into the creative zones both within their organization and within their alliance network. In the network economy, seeking new wealth options on a continuous basis is the challenge. Constantly building and harnessing collaborative competence is the name of the game.

Word to the Wise

For those of you involved in the study or business of formulating and implementing strategy, we have a few final comments.

If you are a manager, you can no longer manage alliances in isolation. Most firms are embedded in some form of network involving varying degrees of commitment. To plan and manage alliances in isolation is to ignore the fact that alliances interact with one another. Actions initiated in isolation can have conflicting or synergistic effects on other alliances connected to your firm.

Consultants or analysts in the business of analyzing situations and providing solutions, have to consider the impact of their recommendations on the network as a whole. To examine actions and prescribe solutions on an individual basis is to ignore the impact and spillover effects of those recommendations on the entire network embedding the firm. While extremely attractive from a dyadic perspective, a recommendation may potentially have serious consequences for the revenues and profitability of the network as a whole, and may move firms from a previously advantageous position within the network to a position of extreme competitive disadvantage.

Chapter 2

E-Alliances: What's New About Them?

John Bell[*]   L24,
L14
L86

Strategic alliances have been popular for at least two decades. In the last one or two years, however, the number of strategic alliances increased exponentially. Most of these alliances are related to the New Economy. The New Economy, characterized by a convergence of industries and a significant role for the Internet, is about to be built up now and in the coming years. Charactistic for this development is the enormous speed with which new Internet-related companies are established and the necessity for firms to redesign their business model.

Strategic alliances play an important role in the creation of The New Economy. The so-called E-alliances or @lliances enable companies to:

- Redesign their business model and tailor it to the cyberspace requirements.
- Learn quickly the necessary skills and know how to act in The New Economy.
- Effectively and efficiently enter new distribution channels (and consequently new (potential) customers).
- Speed up the development of new technologies and standards.
- Be in touch simultaneously with a great diversity of technological developments.

---

[*]The author thanks Dr. Margreet Boersma and Dr. Marc Douma for their comments.

Those who are familiar with strategic alliances might ask themselves: What is the difference with non E-alliances? Regular strategic alliances also enable companies to (re)design their business model, learn other skills and technologies and enter new markets and distributing channels. So what's new about E-alliances?

E-alliances versus "Normal" Alliances

E-alliances have some characteristics which differentiate them from regular strategic alliances. The characteristics of both are shown in Figure 1.

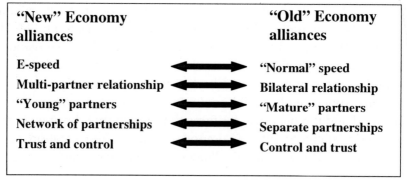

Figure 1.

One of the most remarkable and distinguishing features of E-alliances is the speed with which they are (and need to be) established. The developments on the Internet are going extremely quickly. First-mover advantages do not last very long, as information flows freely over the world wide web. By a simple click of the mouse, a whole webpage can be copied. The imitability of ideas, concepts, and business models is high. Every day a new competitor can harvest on your ideas. Hence, speed is crucial.

Another element which underlines the role of speed is the potential value premium an Internet-related company may receive if it decides to go public. Until the recent capital market correction, most of the so-called Dot.com companies did not make any profits yet, although their value was extremely high. It is uncertain how long this practice will continue. Again, speed is required if one wants to reap the fruits of one's investments in The New Economy.

Strategic alliances are the appropriate mechanisms for realizing the required speed. By cooperating, companies can develop and adopt new technologies, create new business models using the core competencies of their partners, and learn to use their competitive advantages in different areas. Instead of allying, these things can also be obtained through mergers and acquisitions. However, given the inertia inherent to post-merger integration and the reduced flexibility, and the extreme premium value which is accepted on the market, mergers and acquisitions are less attractive mechanisms to meet the need for speed. Companies which choose to develop all skills and know how internally, will most likely be too late.

Both in the "Old" and in the "New" Economy, strategic alliances have these advantages over internal developments and mergers and acquisitions. The main difference, however, is the speed which is imposed by some of the above-mentioned developments. A lack of preparation is a significant reason for the failure of alliances. In the rat race to the New Economy, the time available for preparation becomes shorter, which may have a dramatic effect on the achievement of the intended goals and speed.

A second interesting feature of E-alliances is the use of multiple partners in the relationship. Many of the announced partnerships entail more than two partners. For example, Ford, Daimler Chrysler, GM decided to set up an alliance to combine their on-line purchasing power, while Oracle and Commerce One will take care of the required software. Some other examples are the alliances between Microsoft and 200 E-commerce partners, Cisco with 33 partners, Oracle with 20 partners. This multiple partnership deviates E-alliances from the alliances in the Old Economy where a majority of the partnerships were set up by two partners. Having an alliance on a one-to-one basis already implies a lot of coordination and potential misunderstanding. These issues will aggravate if the number of partners increases.

The contribution of the partners in E-alliances does not seem to vary much from the one in regular alliances. The contribution focuses either on sharing knowledge, providing entry into a new market or distribution channel, setting the industry standard, and so on.

Part of the E-alliances are set up with relatively "young" partners. Young in the sense of the age of the owners of the (Dot.com) company, as well as young in the sense of the number of years the company exists. For example, Oracle has created strategic partnerships with rather new Web services firms and consultancies, including Agency.Com, AnswerThink Consulting Group, iXL, Sapient, US Interactive, and Viant. The relative youth of the owners suggests less experience, which is likely to be compensated by a fresh, and sometimes controversial, view. Large, established companies hired people in the age of 15–25 years to help them develop their E-strategy.

Many Internet-related companies were established in the last one or two years. As such, these companies are still in the entrepreneurial stage and, most likely, do not have a well-defined way of working. This can be an attractive feature in partnering, as possible conflicts because of organizational heritage will be limited.

A fourth distinctive characteristic is that the alliances that are established appear to be chosen from a network perspective. Instead of setting up one strategic alliance with another company (either a competitor, supplier, or customer), more and more companies engage in a great many alliances. IBM, for example, announced alliances with DELL, Nokia, Compaq, Intel, Microsoft, Cisco, Lafayette, and so on. Microsoft created alliances with, amongst others, PricewaterhouseCoopers, 200 e-commerce partners, IBM, and Banyan Systems.

The pace with which all these alliances are announced with all kinds of different partners suggest that a network perspective is used. These companies attempt to build up a good position in The New Economy which is still characterized by high uncertainty. By partnering with many different companies in a diversity of areas, companies can reduce uncertainty and even may be able to (partially) design The New Economy.

The last feature we focus on here is the role of trust and control as coordinating mechanisms. Given the volatility and the velocity of the developments of The New Economy, companies set up alliances with many different partners at a speed which is much higher than before. Being able to manage all these partnerships adequately, and, consequently, try to realize the intended objectives in time, puts a great stress on parent companies. Instead of a heavy focus on the control mode of coordination, the limited available time necessitates companies to change their preferred mode of coordination. In the current situation, trust is a suitable coordination mechanism.

Trust can be a powerful tool which alleviates the simultaneous coordination and management of a great variety of alliances. A more control-oriented focus takes a lot of time, and, as a consequence, will probably hinder the activities and the continuity of a multitude of alliances. The use of trust is a sign of the respect you as a company have for your partner. An essential prerequisite for an effective and successful use of trust is that the partners have an explicit and joint understanding of the objectives of the strategic alliance. Another important issue is that potential cheating is covered adequately by a signed contract.

Conclusions

Based on the comparison described above, we could say that E-alliances share many characteristics with the "regular" strategic alliances. At the same time, there are some specific elements which differentiates them from normal strategic alliances. These elements mainly relate to the pace with which @lliances have to be set up and the observation that @lliances are set up with more than one partner. The remaining three differences as distinguished in Figure 1 are more or less deductible from these two main factors.

To become a successful E-alliance player, firms should build up new alliance capabilities which suit the demands posed in The New Economy. Most of the alliance capabilities required in The Old Economy are likely to prevail, albeit they must be transformed to better meet the need for speed.

Chapter 3

The Corporation Is Dead. . . . Long Live the Constellation!

Benjamin Gomes-Casseres and James Bamford

LI4 G34
L24 D21

Constellations of firms are becoming increasingly popular. However, they can take an enormous variety of different organizational designs. In order to get a better grasp on the design of constellations, this paper identifies four key design variables. By combining these variables, managers can design constellations, which optimally suit their specific situation.

The Challenge of Constellation Design

A few years ago, Cable & Wireless ran a series of glossy advertisements proclaiming that, "The firm is dead. Long live the federation." Great slogan. Too bad the sloganeer was later slayed by the marketplace for never having figured out how to operate a "constellation" — a group of firms linked together through alliances. The lesson of Cable & Wireless is not that firms should abandon the idea of competing in constellations. A better lesson is that astute design and management matters for constellations, just as they do for stand-alone alliances. In fact, effective constellation strategies have become essential to comparative advantage in many modern industries, from global services to e-business.

Many have tried their hand at constellation design. Some constellations are purely contractual. To create momentum for its network computer — and thus displace the constellation around the personal computer — Oracle raced to line up as many supporters as it could through contractual deals. Airlines have experimented with constellations in which a few select partners maintained cross-equity investments in each other and a larger group of partners was linked contractually to the equity core. Early on in the global telecom battles, AT&T followed a similar design blueprint. But in this case, the various equity partners owned shares of a common company, WorldPartners (Figure 1).

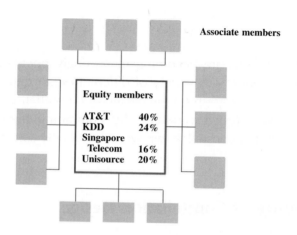

Figure 1. WorldPartners constellation, ca. 1996.

Apart from the choice between equity and non-equity links, the design options are mind-boggling. This is partly because decisions are shaped by industry environments, firm goals, and firm capabilities, all of which exhibit high degrees of variation. Competing in constellations is also a new style of strategy; this means that pioneers are still experimenting and learning daily what to do and what not to do. Like it or not, competition of group versus group is here to stay, and firms need to understand the dynamics of constellation design. The early evidence suggests that design revolves around four broad choices:

• Constellation Size
• Membership Mix

- Internal Rivalry
- Collective Governance

The Size of the Constellation

The total market reach of the group will have a bearing on the success of the group. This is particularly true on two occasions: when seeking a standard or pursuing economies of scale. But choosing an appropriate definition of size is tricky — and will turn on the precise strategy of the constellation. When trying to establish a standard, for instance, the sheer number of partners or the total marketshare of the partners is the best way to measure size. When seeking scale advantages, however, total production capacity of the group or average production capacity per member may be better to aim at. Cable & Wireless missed this distinction. The firm's strategy in designing its global telecommunications constellation was to assemble as many partners from as many countries as possible. Yet neither of these mattered much to global customers, except perhaps its stake in Hong Kong Telecom. Concert, the 1996 joint venture between British Telecom and MCI, was an instant market leader with just two partners. MCI and BT understood that in this arena — providing voice, video, and data services to multinational corporations — competitive advantage hinged on the size and reputation of the lead firms, as well as the nimbleness of the alliance itself. Later, of course, WorldCom would buy MCI, breaking up the BT–MCI alliance, and AT&T jumped at the opportunity to replace MCI in a new Concert alliance, thereby dropping its involvement in WorldPartners.

The Mix of Members

At times, advantage comes from the ability to assemble a diverse set of capabilities. What matters then is not the sizes or the number of pieces but, rather, that the right pieces are assembled snugly together. Composition has been a key to designing constellations in the market for personal digital assistants (PDAs), the little hand-held device which promised the computing power of a simple PC, the communications capability of a cellular phone, and the size, styling, and durability of consumer electronics. To compete in this environment, firms had to deal with the convergence of at least four industries — computer hardware, computer software, telecommunications, and consumer electronics. Major companies in each of these industries entered the field, each arriving with particular strengths. They each assembled firms into constellations, which gave them access to the technical capabilities they lacked. Constellations can also demand geographic diversity. Consider the case of Asia Link, a constellation in the Asian advertising business. Asia Link was composed of firms with very similar sets of capabilities: each had a diverse range of industry experience, $10–$80 million in annual revenue, and a staff of 50–100 professionals. Yet in terms of geographies, the members were intentionally distinct. Each was the leading local firm in one of 11 national markets stretching from Japan to India. By designing for such geographic diversity, the constellation believed it could defend itself against such encroaching global giants as Ogilvy & Mather and Saatchi & Saatchi.

Internal Rivalry

Asia Link is also designed to restrict competition among member firms. Each member was the constellation's only representative in a given national market. One member would make a referral across boundaries, receiving a royalty fee, while continuing to retain that portion of the business left back home. This was not dissimilar to the practice of Japanese keiretsu, where an "exclusion rule" said there should be no duplication of activities among members. Managing internal rivalry is one of the great challenges of large, complex constellations.

But is exclusivity always best? No. Some internal rivalry is, after all, likely to encourage innovation, increase flexibility, and provide a security of supply. And given that member firms remain separate entities, internal competition is inevitable at some level. Therefore, virtually all constellations contain elements of both conflict and collaboration. The microprocessor industry offers an interesting case. By the early 1990s, four constellations had appeared to challenge the preeminence of Intel. The groups were led by HP, IBM, Sun, and Mips, and each was betting that Intel could be challenged by group momentum and a more advanced processing technology, called reduced instruction-set computing (RISC). The fact that the members in each group had this goal in common, however, did not automatically limit their rivalry. And here the various constellations took different approaches. HP explicitly limited rivalry, choosing members for their unique capabilities or markets; but this reduced the number of players it could accept as partners. Sun Microsystems, on the other hand, promoted competition within its group, even encouraging members to compete for the design of next generation chips. By declaring that partners were allowed to clone its machines, Sun believed it could facilitate the spread of its architecture; by pitting chip designers against one another, it would spur innovation.

Mips Computer Systems chose a line somewhere between HP and Sun. Mips encouraged competition, but also contained and segmented it. Its constellation was designed with rings around a core, with internal rivalry intensifying as one moved outward (Figure 2). That core was Mips, which vowed not to compete with its allies, and prevented any from competing with it. Mips would be the constellation's only chip designer, and nothing more. The chip manufacturers — the next ring of the constellation — would be limited to a maximum of six licensed firms. Yet even this competition was compartmentalized, since the semiconductor partners were chosen according to their geographic market strengths. According to Mips president Robert Miller, the aim was to sign on "one of the three semiconductor firms in the United States, one of the top three in Japan, and one of the top three in Europe." The final rings of the constellation were sales and marketing. Here competition flourished. Mips developed relationships with OEMs, distributors, value-added resellers, and systems integrators, and let them create and divide the market.

Which one of these three approaches worked best? While any answer is influenced by the forces external to constellation design, each model had its problems. The HP model limited the spread of the

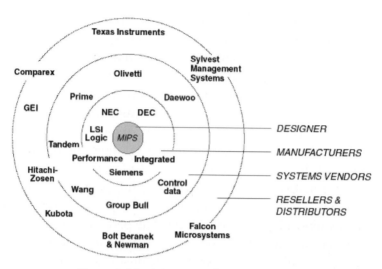

Figure 2. The Mips constellation, ca. 1992.

HP technology; ultimately, HP gave up on its RISC technology and joined with Intel on a joint R&D alliance. Sun clearly benefited from having many potential chip vendors, but this competition tended to benefit only Sun, not the group as a whole. Also, Sun found the competition from the clone makers too much to handle. Fearing that they would undercut its own hardware business, Sun ordered its value-added resellers to stop selling Sun clones. The Sun constellation survives, but with Sun in a much more central and controlling position than the original design implied. The Mips constellation, in one sense, also failed. Having a small firm like Mips at the center of a massive constellation created real coordination problems and led to a partial disintegration of the group. Mips was eventually acquired by Silicon Graphics, one of its early partners, who had grown dependent on the Mips-designed chips for its workstations.

Thus, the most effective constellations seem to create an organizational structure, which promotes collaboration rather than competition. But this is not to suggest squashing all internal competition. Internal rivalry can usually be managed during sales and marketing, while it is highly problematic during research and development. Also, competition works best when it does not involve the lead firm: there is a certain clarity of purpose gained from having the leader above the fray, able to arbitrate in the best interests of the group.

Collective Governance

A constellation doesn't have to have a governing body with voting rights for every member. Boeing has no such mechanism for its vast supplier network, nor does IBM for its network of software developers. However, some form of collective governance is useful when a constellation is large and when it has a high degree of internal competition. The governance mechanism allows partners to establish common goals and rules of behavior — something virtually impossible to do informally. Broadly, there are three types of governance structures for alliance constellations:

- **The General Assembly.** The "United Nations" approach to member management may be useful when the number of partners is large, when multiple capabilities are being assembled, when there is no clear dominant firm, or when the dominant firm wants to downplay its leadership role. The first and last of these were the primary reasons behind the construction of the AT&T global alliance. WorldPartners had an intricate web of staff, committees, and meetings all of which encouraged information exchange among members. Despite these advantages, the general assembly can be slow moving, lack an aggressive, differentiated edge, and require immense amounts of energy to manage. These, too, were characteristics of WorldPartners.
- **The Equity Core.** A tighter governance structure might be one where equity links tie key constellation members together, leaving others floating in a rather unstructured orbit. Such an approach is useful when there is a defined core group, and when these partners are similar types of firms (but not direct competitors). Delta Air Lines built an equity core for its global marketing alliance in the early 1990s, exchanging small but important cross-equity stakes with its two main partners, Swissair and Singapore Airlines. These three

integrated strategy at each board meeting. On the periphery, each firm maintained its own network of partners. There are drawbacks. First, the equity core provides very little coordination among the total network membership. In other words, a Delta partner such as Virgin Atlantic had no real relationship with Singapore Airlines, much less with one of Singapore's partners. Second, the equity-core model may also pose real limits to growth. If entry into the center of the constellation requires an equity ante, there are simply a limited number of firms, which can participate. Indeed, the Delta–Swissair–Singapore alliance was overtaken by larger constellations, such as the Star Alliance, which did not use the equity-core model.

- **The Dominant Firm.** This is the most common constellation structure, if only because it requires the least amount of conscious coordination among leading players. Typically, a large firm like GM, Boeing, or IBM will stand up, lay out a strategic direction for the constellation, and invite others to trot along behind. This was the design advocated by Bank of America back in the 1960s for its BankAmericard credit card association. The dominant firm provides the other members with some important advantages: perhaps large and guaranteed volumes, adjudication of disputes, discipline of unwieldy members. Of course, it can lead to excesses. As the members of the BankAmericard association discovered, the lead firm can make decisions, which enrich it at the expense of the others. Also, the dominant firm model simply cannot be applied in many instances. Delta simply could not dominate its global alliance the way Bank of America sought to: its size and reach are not large enough.

Whatever the formal governance structure, the collective has to have some way of coordinating actions. Without leadership or an agreed-upon formula for making joint decisions, a constellation cannot be expected to formulate and execute a consistent strategy. Instead, internal divisions and differences in perspectives among members will most likely pull the constellation in different directions. An analogy from American Wild West is apt: out in the barren plains, cowboys would tie their horses to each other at night, knowing that each horse would pull in a different direction and the group would go nowhere. An alliance group without leadership and collective governance will be no different.

Chapter 4

Does Alliance Management Differ from Network Management?

Daisy Geurts and Han van der Zee

L14

L24

For several reasons, among which the increasing demand from customers for complex end-to-end solutions and the increasing tendency of suppliers to focus on their core competencies, we observe a shift from the use of bilateral alliances towards the setting up of networks. Alliances are bilateral agreements between two firms, aiming to develop new markets or technologies. Networks on the other hand may consist of a very large number of partners and therefore exhibit some different dynamics. As networks differ from alliances in more than one respect, the question arises whether networks require a different kind of management. From the research project "Competing for Partners",[1] in which nine partnerships were researched, among which several alliances and networks, we conclude that the answer to this question must be yes. Networks require a distinctively different management approach than alliances.[2] The six most important differences between alliance management and network management are summarized in Table 1.

---

[1] The research project "Competing for Partners" has been carried out by the Nolan Norton Institute. A complete report can be found in De Man, Van der Zee and Geurts (2000). This report describes the cases used in this article in more detail as well.
[2] As there are different types of alliances and networks, these different types of management as well. For alliances this has been clarified by Anand and Khanna (2000); for management of different network types see De Man, Geurts and Van Dullemen (2001).

Table 1. Key differences between alliance management and network management.

	Alliances	Networks
1 Dominant party	None, equality	One dominant partner (or group of partners), who initiates and stimulates
2 Planning	Joint business planning and joint results	Influencing and lobbying
3 Evaluation	Based on impact in market and balance between input/output	Based on realization of common vision and balance between input/output
4 Management responsibility	Alliance management	Dominant partner and management of partner firms
5 Managing expectations	By defining new opportunities and joint business planning	By confirming social relations, keeping up the Feel Good Factor and having common discussions and meetings
6 Change process	Planned, phased based	Fluid, only limited control

Dominant Party

In bilateral alliances, there often is no dominant partner. Instead, there is equality between the partners. This equality may be embodied in formal structures. Examples of these are agreements on sharing investments and revenues, equal participation in equity joint ventures or both partners having an equal number of seats on the alliance board.

In networks, complete equality of all partners in management of the network would slow down decision-making processes to the point of creating inertia. The more partners are involved, the more complicated the decision-making process becomes. Therefore, management of the network is often left to one partner (Gomes Casseres, 1994) or a small core team, who stimulates the rest of the network, initiates renewal and changes and, in general, manages the progress of the network towards its goals. This is not necessarily a formalized way of working, but may emerge in practice.

The differences as mentioned can be illustrated by two examples. The first example is the alliance between Cisco and KPMG, established in 1999 to leverage KPMG's worldwide consulting and solution development expertise and Cisco's leadership in infrastructure solutions. Together, they will develop innovative, repeatable solutions that will create compelling value for their clients. This alliance's activities include knowledge transfer (to achieve leadership in network technologies), solution development (to define innovative business solutions for the Internet), business development (to attract new clients and new business opportunities) and marketing (to undertake joint campaigns and events and to leverage Cisco's market dominance in the Internet). Equality in the partnership is embodied in a mutual high investment in the alliance (a large financial investment from Cisco and a commitment by KPMG to hire 4000 consultants). Also, both partners have strong alliance management teams, which create a balance of power in the alliance.

For the second example, we can zoom in on the WAP Forum network, established to set the standard on mobile Internet. The Wireless Application Protocol (WAP) enables the use of a mobile device for a number of high-bandwidth services like transferring money between bank accounts, surfing the Internet or checking whether you left the lights on back home. The mission of the WAP Forum is to promote the use and development of the WAP technology. Companies that stand to benefit from increasing use of mobile phones developed the technology and sales of related equipment. In 1997, Ericsson, Nokia, Motorola and Phone.com set up the WAP Forum to further develop the WAP technology into an industry standard. Right now, the Forum consists of the four founding members, 150 full members (technology partners) and 70 associate members (content partners, like Amazon). The WAP Forum operates in many respects like a virtual organization. It has no profit objective. There are a number of bodies involved in the management of the network, illustrating the importance of a small core team that initiates and stimulates the network. The management structure of the WAP Forum is presented in Figure 1. There is a WAP Forum

Board of Directors (13 members), responsible for setting up and disbanding working groups within the network, specifying working group deliverables and publishing the final WAP specifications. The Specification Committee acts as the WAP's project manager. It is responsible for implementing the board's decisions, setting priorities within and among the working groups and monitoring of the working groups' progress. There is an architecture group to manage the content of the WAP standard and there are working groups to carry out the actual work of defining standards. The founding members are *qualitate qua* members of the board and are the most active participants in the other working groups. In this way they guide and manage the network. Despite this structure of decision-making and the considerable control exercised by the founding members, the WAP Forum is still characterized by extensive discussions and relatively democratic decision-making. Although the impressive number of partners in the network slows down decision-making, without the activities of the core group of founding members the network would probably grind to a halt.

Networks need a small management team, like in the WAP Forum case, because of the necessity to keep the network manageable and to guarantee its progress. Who is included in the core team differs per

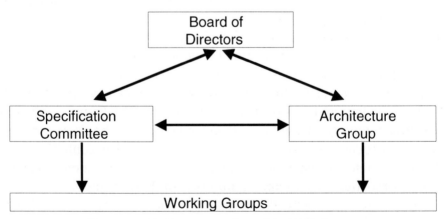

Figure 1. Management structure of the WAP Forum.
(Copyright: WAP Forum Ltd)

network. In the WAP Forum, it is the founding members; in other networks, they may be the most innovative partners or partners whose interest in the network is more strategic than others. They may want to adapt the speed of decision-making and progress in the network to their own internal speed or exert a relatively big influence on the processes inside the network.

Planning and Evaluation

The larger number of partners in a network also influences the planning and evaluation processes. In alliances the two partners may use relatively straightforward joint planning and evaluation mechanisms, using management tools like business plans or scorecards. In networks the larger number of partners inhibits a simple and transparent planning and evaluation process, often leading to the use of informal and qualitative mechanisms for management control (Jones, Hesterly, Borgatti, 1997).

As has been described above, joint business planning and striving for joint results is embodied in the formulation of the goals of the KPMG–Cisco alliance: they will jointly develop innovative, repeatable end-to-end-solutions. KPMG and Cisco will notify each other on their engagements, involve each other in client proposals etc. Apart from this, KPMG and Cisco do not use joint detailed planning and control mechanisms. They only measure and reports results from the alliance (e.g. turnover from the alliance) for their own organizations and have not defined indicators like joint sales targets.

Alliances generally become more flexible over time, once the partners have experienced success in their partnership. In an alliance, there is generally room for partners to broaden the scope of their shared activities over time. In networks, the objectives and scope are also defined, but more in terms of intentions and vision than in measurable targets. Getting all partners in a network to agree on a change of scope or objectives is obviously more difficult and time-consuming than in an alliance. In this regard, networks seem to have a certain kind of implicit inertia (Grabher, 1990).

Evaluation of alliances is based on the impact of the alliance in the marketplace, because alliances often start with a clear set of predefined and measurable goals: setting up a new business, developing a market or delivering an end-to-end offering to existing and new customers (like KPMG–Cisco). The progress towards that goal is relatively easy to measure. Networks, on the other hand, often define an overall goal or vision (like standardization) and subsequently define several projects to reach that goal. Measures of success in networks are not as quantitative as they are in alliances. For example, how can one measure the realization of the common vision? A similarity in the evaluation process in networks and alliances is the fact that partners evaluate the partnerships based on the balance between input and output. Partners make an assessment of the question whether sufficient revenues from that partnership compensate the investments in the partnership. This assessment may comprise quite some qualitative issues.

Management Responsibility

Alliances are usually managed by alliance managers who are responsible for the performance of the alliances under their control (Harbison and Pekar, 1998). In the KPMG–Cisco alliance, both parties have installed alliance management teams. The KPMG alliance management team has a number of roles, including managing the contacts with the partner, strategic planning of joint initiatives, supporting KPMG-directors to implement the alliance. Cisco has put a similar structure in place. This includes the appointment of a senior vice president of global alliances and the formation of a Cisco alliance team. In networks, the existence of a dominant partner is reflected in the management responsibility structure. Management responsibility is borne by the dominant partner(s), who allocates more resources (time, people, and funds), to the network than other partners.

Managing Expectations

Alliances and networks have in common that managing the expectations of the partners is an important aspect of keeping the partnership together.

Partnerships benefit from shared mindsets, norms and values, and a common understanding on the future opportunities, costs and payoffs. The way in which expectations are managed differs between networks and alliances. In alliances, the joint planning process provides clarity on future possibilities of the partnership. By defining new opportunities and jointly assessing the risks, the partners develop a common understanding on their common future. Hence, management of expectations takes place in a formal manner and is defined as a separate activity.

In a network, managing the expectations is even more important because of the large number of partners and the differences in speed, initiative, information and management responsibility between the partners. The relatively informal and unstructured nature of the planning process requires other tools for managing expectations than are used in alliances. Network meetings are important in this. It turns out that although these meeting are organized to discuss content issues, they also serve to confirm the social relations within the network and to keep up the "Feel-Good-Factor". By means of intense interaction, expectations on the development of the network are exchanged and confirmed. WAP Forum meetings take place six to eight times a year. During these meetings, the members work on content and implicitly on relationship development as well. Consequently, managing expectations is much more an informal process, intertwined with normal network activities.

Change Process

Partnerships are in no way static. They develop over time. Relationships can intensify or weaken, new partners can be attracted, contracts revised and governance structures adapted (Reuer and Zollo, 2000). The way in which the change process is managed differs between alliances and networks. Change in the sense of exit and entrance of partners in an alliance is quite difficult, whereas in a network this is relatively easy. The underlying reason for this difference is that alliances usually exhibit a higher level of integration in a narrower scope of activities than networks. A much greater challenge is posed by changing the goals and directions of the partnership. In particular in networks, where the number of partners is large, obtaining agreement on a change of strategy is almost impossible.

Change management is an important topic for the alliances studied in our research. For KPMG and Cisco, the different phases in the formation of the alliance are carefully planned and managed and executed with great speed and perseverance. The way change management takes place in networks is completely different. Some networks evolve over time, seemingly unmanaged and unstructured — change seems just to have happened. But the importance of the core team's ambitions in the change of the network must not be underestimated. Although there is no partner with formal and direct control over the network, the core members certainly play a key role in initiating changes in the network. The difference with alliances is that all parties exert only limited control, which makes the change process more fluid and less planned.

Conclusion

Alliances and networks require different management approaches. It would be a mistake to assume that once a capability in managing in alliances has been built up, a firm is also able to function effectively in its network as well. Managing networks requires a different approach. In networks the emphasis lies on qualitative, informal and relational aspects, whereas in alliances managers can make use of some quantitative, formal and structural management tools and approaches. Firms may give up some control in alliances, but in networks they have to do so to a much larger extent. This requires managers to change their mental models of management and to develop a network mindset (Van der Zee, 2000). Without a network attitude, firms will not be able to benefit from being embedded in a network.

References

Anand, B., and T. Khanna, 2000, "*Do firms learn to create value? The case of alliances*", *Strategic Management Journal*, vol. 21, pp. 295–315.

De Man, A.P., D. Geurts and G. van Dullemen, 2001, "*Working Networks*", in: H. van der Zee and J. Strikwerda (eds.), *Capturing Value from the New Economy*, Amsterdam, Addison-Wesley (forthcoming).

De Man, A.P., H. van der Zee and D. Geurts, 2000, *Competing for Partners*, Prentice Hall, Amsterdam.

Gomes Casseres, B., 1994, "Group versus group: How alliance networks compete", *Harvard Business Review*, July/August, pp. 62–74.

Grabher, G., 1990, *The Embedded Firm*, London, Routledge.

Harbison, J.R., and P. Pekar, 1998, *Institutionalising Alliance Skills*, Los Angeles, Booz Allen & Hamilton.

Jones, C., W.S. Hesterly and S.P. Borgatti, 1997, "A General theory of network governance: Exchange conditions and social mechanisms", *Academy of Management Review*, vol. 22, no. 4, pp. 911–945.

Reuer, J., and M. Zollo, 2000, "Managing governance adaptations in strategic alliances", *European Management Journal*, vol. 18, no. 2, pp. 164–172.

Van der Zee, H., 2000, "Transformatie van traditionele modellen naar virtuele bedrijfsnetwerken", *Informatie*, October, pp. 32–39.

Chapter 5

The Laws of Alliance Formation

Carlos García-Pont

L 14
L 24

Alliances are at the center of most firms' strategies nowadays. Only recently, BBVA (Banco Bilbao Vizcaya Argentaria) and Telefónica established an alliance to develop financial e-business. These two firms are among the most powerful firms in Spain. Their international expansion has been growing all throughout South America. They are now among the largest multinationals in the South American continent. At the same time, the biggest rival of BBVA, BSCH (Banco Santander Central Hispano) is participating in the take over of Natwest by Royal Bank of Scotland. These are two very different moves by to direct rivals with the same home base.

This is the rule more than the exception. It is clear that whichever industry you are in, you cannot avoid playing the alliance game. The perspective has changed in the last years. Perhaps ten or twenty years ago one had to justify to ones stakeholders that an alliance was being created. Nowadays, a firm has to justify not participating in the myriad of alliance networks that are being formed in most industries. However, alliances are only part of the picture. The dynamics within and across industries also include mergers and acquisitions that are transforming industries. Furthermore, in the early 90s we concentrated on "within industry" alliances. Those were reshaping the industry structure in such industries as automobiles, automobile components and airlines. Today, an increasing number of alliances cut across traditional definitions of industry. The one mentioned above between BBVA and Telefó nica is a good example.

This alliance phenomenon places two major challenges on firms: firstly, firms have to learn the rules of alliance formation and, secondly, management of firms themselves has to change.

The Rules of Alliance Formation

In order to be able to play the alliance game, managers have to identify the rules that govern the formation of an alliance network. It is clear that firms cannot pick their cooperative strategy in isolation. They are embedded in a network of corporate relationships that influence the available options for each one of the firms in the network. Every time an alliance is formed, the relative competitive positions in an industry change. This in turn changes every firm's position as a potential partner. That also happens with your own moves. With every alliance you constrain your future possibilities in forming other partnerships. Understanding the laws that govern alliance dynamics becomes an important strategic tool. Three laws of alliance formation can be found (see Figure 1).

The first law that seems to regulate the dynamics of alliance formation is the first mover advantage. In telecom, banking, autos, pharmaceuticals, airlines, semiconductors, computers, software and other industries there seems to be a triggering event that provokes a move by a first mover. Once an industry leader moves, followers do not want to be left out of the game. This is especially important in industries with a small number of competitors or industries where there

---

First Law
First mover advantage and imitation shape strategic blocks.
Second law
Membership of strategic block is likely to be exclusive.
Third law
Alliance networks are a response to an imperfect market for strategic capabilities (viz. uncertainty about the future).

Figure 1. Laws of alliance formation.

are clearly defined groups of competitors with similar market focus. In this way, Ford established linkages with Mazda, GM with Toyota and Chrysler with Mitsubishi. Oneworld or the Star Alliance are groups of airlines trying to cover the whole world with their flight destinations. Airline customers can move from one airline to the other for continuing the trip. Alliances within the airline industry have grouped competitors in "strategic blocks", which are groups of firms that collectively try to match the collective capabilities of another group of firms. Strategic block formation also preceded consolidation in the auto industry and in the European banking industry. It looks that one of the laws regulating the dynamics of network formation are those of informed imitation, where firms study and match the movements of other firms (Osborn, 1999). Consequently, a powerful first mover defines the sequence of alliances that are going to be formed. It is the first mover who chooses how alliances are going to improve its competitive position. But it is never too late to be a first mover. Different dynamics overlap each other, and you can always be a first mover in a different alliance game.

The second law that seems to regulate the dynamics of network formation is the law of exclusivity. In different words, you cannot be the friend of my enemy. That is, transitivity implies that firms group themselves into blocks more or less irreversibly linked (alliances vs., merges or acquisitions) to each other. Membership in a strategic block does preclude a firm from membership in a different strategic block. However there seems to be a certain tolerance. As long as the linkage that is established with a third firm does not conflict with the objectives of the block, a firm might be linked with firms outside its own block. Studies have shown that firms tied to a common third party are more likely to establish a link between them (Gulati, 1995).

The third law is that of market imperfections. I like to think of alliances and other forms of firm linkages as the result of a market for strategic assets in a turbulent world. The speed of change to which today's markets are subjected, creates a huge deal of uncertainty in terms of which are the best strategic activities for competing in present markets. Furthermore it creates uncertainty regarding which are the product/markets that are going to be the future. Firms cannot internally adapt to these strategic options at the required speed and do have to buy or rent the strategic capabilities that are needed to pursue those market opportunities (Nohria and García Pont, 1991). Thus, the formation of alliance networks is a response to an imperfect market for strategic capabilities. Continuously reshaping the strategic capabilities of the firm to match the needs of the ever-changing business has become an impossible task. Every firm has to incorporate or gain access to the complementary capabilities of other firms in order to be able to respond to the demands of a continuously changing marketplace.

Changes in Management

Once the firm becomes a full player in an alliance network, its basic configuration changes. Firms have traditionally managed major value chain activities within their hierarchical or administrative control. When they are involved in a number of alliances that is not necessarily true. Increasingly a number of activities are outside their direct control. They are done with or by their partners. Firms have to readapt to the realities of managing a multiplex of relationships with other third parties who themselves are embedded in their own network of relationships. This brings me to the second point: participation in alliances changes the way firms have to be managed.

The result of this myriad of alliances is that the organization of firms has to change. Academics have traditionally argued that firms are open organizations that relate to the different environmental conditions where they perform their activities. This dimension of openness has changed. It is not only the environment that plays a role, it is the number of contacts that firms have with outside legal entities which changes the conception of a firm. A firm is a modular concept. Value chains, the complete set of operations that configure a business, may incorporate different sets of legal entities with different shareholders. Moreover, a firm will participate in different groupings depending on the business or the activity it has at hand. This implies a difference in philosophy. The number of individuals within a firm that has contact with outside constituents multiplies as the number of alliances for different purposes increase. Coordination between these multiple constituent activities becomes increasingly reliant on these individuals. The level of empowerment and delegation has to increase. In this way, firms have only parts of the pieces of the puzzle that configure their total value chain and the network of relationships within the firms opens up to the partners. Up to 50% of the key relationships of first line managers within a business can be with external constituents. This certainly imposes new challenges in the division and coordination of tasks. Command and control styles of management are continuously challenged.

From a manager's point of view, the percentage of his working time spent inside his own firm, decreases. In a way, normative ways of managing his actions become more important. Managers have to become entrepreneurs within their own sphere of action, but also have to take into account the interest of their partners. As a consequence, firms need not only to adapt their internal operations to the requirements of alliances, but have to think about the way they are going to relate to their partners as well. This requires them to develop an expertise in managing really open organizations.

Summary

The increase in alliance activity forces firms to grasp the rules that underpin the formation of alliances. It also requires managers to change the management of their firms towards an open and entrepreneurial style, which takes account of the interests of alliance partners.

References

Gulati, R., 1995, "Social structure and alliance form ation patterns", *Administrative Science Quarterly*, vol. 40, no. 4; pp. 619–652.

Nohria, N. and C, García-Pont 1991. "Global strategic linkages and industry structure", *Strategic Management Journal*, vol. 12. Special Summer Issue on Global Strategy, pp. 105–124.

Osborn, R., G. Johannes, G. Denekamp and C. C. Baughn, "*The institutionalization of Industry Alliance Configurations*". Paper presented in the Alliance Network Conference at IESE, Barcelona, Spain.

Chapter 6

Preemptive[1] Alliances in the E-Economy©

Larraine Segil

Preemptive alliances in the e-economy abound:

- AT&T's acquisition of TCI set their preemptive positioning in the cable/ telecommunications world.
- AOL's preemptive acquisition of Time Warner set their new position in the brick and mortar world.
- Cisco grabs independent software vendors to gain ground with US small businesses and improve their e-commerce capabilities.
- Mannesmann has established a relationship with AOL Europe that preempts an AOL attack by forming a strategic alliance up front.

In this article the concept of preemptive alliances is defined and managerial issues related to this specific alliance type are discussed.

What Is a Preemptive Alliance?

Although there may be a positive result for both companies, the real motive behind a preemptive alliance is for one or more of the partners to preempt a competitor. That is to say, the grabber (Company X) is

---

[1]Preemptive alliances is a servicemark of Larraine Segil.

grabbing a grabbee (Company Y) in such a way that Company X will preempt any competitor from partnering with Company Y in that particular application or market space.

This effectively takes Company Y out of the competitive play and inserts them into the Company X network of partners. The result is a different strategic positioning for the connected companies and possibly a new set of market dynamics for all players to contemplate.

Microsoft has made an art of preemptive alliances — such as its alliance with PointCast, a provider of news and advertising to computers when the users' screens are idle. In aligning with Microsoft, PointCast was to integrate Microsoft's web browser into its product offering to displace Netscape. Until that time, Netscape had provided Internet software for PointCast. In addition, PointCast accessed MSNBC and other Microsoft properties for content. A PointCast channel also appears in the screen of computers using the Microsoft Window's operating system. While this alliance added value for PointCast, it was clearly a winning, preemptive move for Microsoft in its duel for Internet dominance.

Why Are Preemptive Alliances Different from Other Alliances?

The main difference is that preemptive partners are generally not good partners. A purely preemptive play will bring a partner to the table who delivers access, size and market share. What preemptive partners often don't deliver, however, are some of the capabilities and resources that are essential to the management of effective partnerships. These include:

- conflict resolution skills;
- detailed and effective metrics;
- careful team selection and modification as the partnership evolves;
- concern for adding incremental value to the partnership over time;
- a consistent commitment to mutuality.

Why Is This Kind of Alliance Particularly Important Today?

Preemptive alliances have been used for decades, generally in the form of acquisitions. The reasons often had to do with control, and those acquired were many times taken out of the market altogether or morphed into organizations that dominated a certain market position. In today's e-economy however, the role of the preemptive alliance has reached a fine art as a tool that enables the grabber to move fast and decisively.

What Are the Downsides of a Preemptive Alliance for the Grabbee?

Preemptive alliances raise the barriers to entry or expansion. But for a small company which is a partner to a larger company's preemptive moves, they can also raise the potential of premature termination or a messy exit — being left behind in the rush for the next preemptive strike by a powerful partner. There is no doubt that the access and market share that Microsoft made available to PointCast were hugely influential and strategic.

However, it was also clear that leveraging that opportunity would be the responsibility of PointCast and that Microsoft would move on to larger and better things.

In this way Microsoft has been able to create huge networks of interlocking relationships worldwide in a multitude of industries — many times entering into these arrangements before Sun Microsystems, Oracle or other potential competitors. In fact, Microsoft has played the game of the "the invisible competitor" and done it well. The invisible competitor is a company outside of an industry who uses the preemptive alliance approach to place a stake in a new industry and immediately become a player. Microsoft has done this in publishing, wireless, telecommunications, and a variety of other industries blurring the boundaries of its "traditional" market so that this word has no meaning. "Market" for Microsoft means everywhere and the preemptive alliance is the method and tool necessary to get there.

Another series of "invisible competitor" preemptive alliances are seen in Europe. Deutsche Bank in March 2000 announced a pan European e-commerce bank with mobile telephone provider Mannesmann (its stock went up 5% when it did!) — this opens the door not only to telecommunications companies to become "invisible competitors" but also to supermarket chains, utilities, automobile manufacturers and others who are moving into cyberbanking. All of these companies have the capability to process money (in the past the purview of banks) and some savvy executives (like those at Spanish Banco Bilbao Vizcaya Argentaria in their deal with Telefonica) are preempting their competitors in jumping into e-commerce alliances as fast as possible. French and Italian banks and their telecom companies have announced similar deals. They involve small cross equity stakes, and cross marketing and the fundamental shift of power from a single vertical industry player, to one that reaches over multiple industries and geographies. In the e-business it's smart to do preemptive alliances fast![2]

The grabbee companies in preemptive alliances however run the risk that their market-heavy partner may decide to become a competitor. The question they must consider is this: How will the grabber manage the alliance? The answer depends on the level of priority the grabber places on this alliance. This is what I call the "project personality".[3]

The criteria for project personalities are summarized in Figure 1. Project Personality is the priority placed on the alliance by the partners. It does not have to be the same although some companies prefer that it be of similar project priority to all partners, or they will not enter the relationship. Corning is one such company that prefers the level of commitment by their partners to equal theirs, especially in joint ventures. Other companies, such as USAA (a US based insurance company

---

[2]See "Fastalliances.com™; Business Development for E-Business" (Wiley, pub date December 1, 2000) by Larraine Segil.

[3]See "Intelligent Business Alliances" (Times Books, Random House) 1996, by Larraine Segil, Chapter 2 on Partner Compatibility and the Mindshift™ Approach to managing cultural differences between partner companies and individual partner managers and also managing differing project priorities.

BET THE FARM	MIDDLE-OF-THE-ROAD	EXPERIMENTAL
Project is integral to the future survival of the organization Part of macro/long term strategy Well financed Senior management is involved	Project is important but not the primary strategy Part of mid term strategy Initial senior management interest wanes unless it becomes a high growth project	Project of limited importance to whole organization but vital to some (e.g. R&D) Resources are committed but limited time/results Conflict resolution mechanisms not well designed

COPYRIGHT: LARRAINE SEGIL 2000 ©

Figure 1. Project Personalities.

primarily for US veterans and their families) is perfectly willing to partner with companies where the project priority for the partner is far higher than for USAA. They do that all the time with suppliers for whom USAA may be their largest (Bet the Farm) customer. They assist their supplier alliance partners to become more professional at partnering[4] by setting high quality standards, metrics and partnership monitoring processes.

Obviously, for PointCast this alliance was of paramount importance. It was "Bet the Farm" because the alliance is integral to the future survival and strategic positioning of the company. As such, the grabbee PointCast devoted excellent resources — time, human, and financial capital — to making sure the alliance is positioned for success.

Preemptive alliances typically do not carry the same priority for the grabber. In most cases, the alliances are likely to be considered "Experimental" or perhaps even less than experimental (extremely low priority) in terms of importance within the organization. By their very nature, experimental alliances may create interest in the initial stages

---

[4]See American Productivity and Quality Center, Houston, Texas, the first Benchmarking Study on Sales and Marketing Alliances, 1998 designed by Larraine Segil as the subject matter expert on Alliances.

of alliance development but should conflict arise, the grabber will be unlikely to resolve it, and will withdraw or lose interest in the alliance. This being the case, grabbers are apt to devote very limited resources to its implementation and will expect to see concrete results in a short amount of time.

What Can Smaller Companies Do to Enhance the Likelihood of Success of Preemptive Alliances?

The incompatibility of project priorities for preemptive alliances will greatly inhibit their chances for success. Every aspect of the alliance is affected by the Project Personality (priority) Type — from negotiating the specifics of the deal, to choosing managers to run the alliance, and, most important, following-up and gaining continuing commitment from the partners.

Without the relatively comparable devotion of all partners, a lopsided alliance must, at the very least, have the commitment by the party for whom the project priority is highest. This partner must commit the major share of time and resources for conflict resolution to the ongoing management of the alliance. Otherwise, the relationship has no real chance for success. Conversely, this means that partnerships where there is a vast difference between the priorities of the partners, CAN be highly successful – however ONLY if the partner for whom the project priority is highest, does all the work. That means not only their work, but potentially the work of all the OTHER partners too. This may mean, at their expense, placing their employees in the other partner's location in order to undertake many of the tasks required to make the partnership successful, or training their partners' employees as part of the commitment.

There are steps smaller start-up companies should take to protect their investments when partnering with well-established companies. While senior management at the smaller company needs to make sure that the project will not be ignored, they must realize that there is a defined time within which progress must be made or funds will be cut.

They must also move into the alliance with a clear understanding that there will be acute pressure to perform until the concept has been proven. They should maintain high levels of communication with and make frequent visits to the larger partner company, observing their action or lack of it, and filling the gaps where necessary, finding short cuts to approval cycles in order not to be overwhelmed by the amount of paperwork that may be required until the project grows and proves its worth.

What Legal Structures Can Be Used?

The methodology for preemptive alliances can utilize multiple legal structures. The most successful preemptors will do just that. If relying only on acquisitions as the primary legal structure, the upside is control in a world where stock as currency makes sense. The downside is that the integration of the entity may be costly and if it is not done efficiently or according to a formula, (as Cisco has been so adept at doing); this could diminish the effectiveness of the preemptive nature of the move. The result may mean that the pace of deal making slows down due to the demands and need for focus on the details of integration. In addition, shareholder perception may be that more than a few acquisitions will cause significant indigestion unless the company has a proven acquisition process and is in a rising market. (Again, Cisco falls into this category.)

Growing markets enable acquirers of all types (including those with preemptive designs) to hide many mistakes. This is similar to the economics of real estate. You have to be fairly incompetent to lose money when real estate prices are going up. It takes real skill, however, to make money when prices are going down. Similarly with acquisitions, when markets are growing, it is relatively simple to make multiple acquisitions because redundancy can be hidden under increasing revenues. Yet, in times of intense competitive consolidation, skill is involved in stripping out the chaff and leaving the precious wheat behind.

Exclusive distribution and licensing arrangements also make sense in the preemptive arena. Even if the window of exclusivity is narrow, in times of increased change, every market is fluid — and the first in, will generally have an advantage. That is why entering the market with a solution that fails is a no-recovery play. Hence, grabbers should be vigilant that their preemptive move is the right one with the best target. AOL made a bold move in their Time Warner acquisition. Certainly, the content and access of both companies would have made Time Warner an attractive property for Yahoo or another ISP. It appears that the move was the right legal structure for AOL because nothing else would have had the same impact or guaranteed control in a similar way.

Should you become a Grabber? Do you have the size, the market share, the process and the guts to take the risk (either capital/stock/human)? Or can you afford NOT to? I speak to over 30,000 executives annually in North America, Asia, Latin America and Europe and my research into this subject shows that more than 58% of them are involved in grabber-type situations. That number is growing. When e-business companies are asked, the numbers are much higher — over 71%. The preemptive alliance approach should be part of every company's portfolio of alliance methodologies, especially for this exploding time of opportunity in the new economy.

Chapter 7

The Future of Alliance Capability: Towards a Basic Necessity for Firm Survival?

L 14
L 24

Ard-Pieter de Man

What Is an Alliance Capability?

There is a vast difference between the alliance performance of firms. On average alliance failure rates of 60 or 70% are not exceptional (KPMG, 1996). Successful firms however can have success rates of 90%, whereas unsuccessful firms can have success rates as low as 30% (Booz Allen & Hamilton, 1998). Likewise the top 25 firms of the Fortune 500 most active in alliances, clearly outperform their competitors in terms of return on equity (see Figure 1). This clear difference between individual firms in their alliance performance suggests that some firms are better able to manage their alliances than others are, and that this may lead to superior financial performance. This observation has led an increasing number of researchers and managers to direct their attention to the subject of alliance capability. An alliance capability can be defined as the ability of a firm to manage its alliances successfully towards achieving their goals.

The attention for building up alliance capabilities is a marked shift away from the traditional approach to alliances (see Figure 2). The traditional approach tried to explain alliance success and failure by focusing on the alliance itself. Issues researched were the structure of the co-operation, the type of contract and the strategic, organizational and cultural fit between the partners forming the alliance.

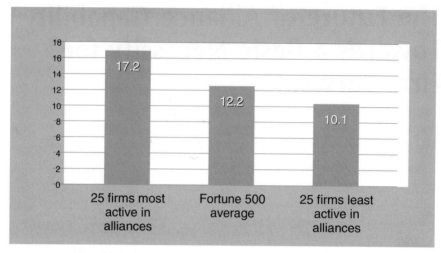

Source: Booz Allen & Hamilton, 1997

Figure 1. Effect of alliance intensity on return on equity.

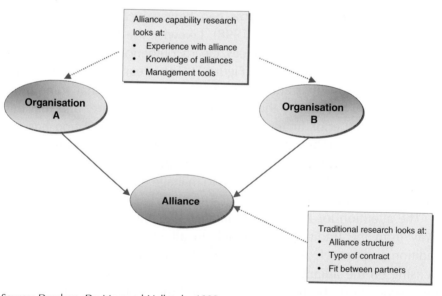

Source: Draulans, De Man and Volberda, 1999

Figure 2. Alliance capability versus the traditional approach.

Alliance capability focuses on the internal organization of the alliance partners and the accumulation of alliance knowledge inside the individual organization. It studies the experience firms have with alliances (Gulati, 1999), the knowledge they have built up about them and the alliance management tools they have implemented. In short: not the relationship is studied, but the ability of the individual partners to manage the relationship. The idea lying behind this approach is that a firm's alliance success will augment when its internal organization is geared for alliance management. The reverse side of this idea may be less obvious, but may be true as well: some of the most important barriers to alliance success lie in the individual partners, not in the co-operation itself.

How Can an Alliance Capability Be Built Up?

At first, preliminary research into the use of alliance training, alliance specialists and different methods of evaluating alliances, found that these management tools had a clearly discernible impact on alliance performance (Draulans, De Man and Volberda, 1999). This supports the hypothesis that firms can learn how to manage alliances. There are several tools firms can use to structure this learning (see Table 1) and to make existing knowledge available to employees.

However, the availability of tools is not a sufficient condition for bringing about an alliance capability. The experience of individuals and the attitude of employees towards alliances are at the core of such a capability. Gaining practical alliance management experience should become a standard element in management careers, if an alliance capability is to be built up. Even more than implementing tools, this will ensure an alliance mindset inside the firm. In practice many firms view alliances as an add-on to existing business, which can be managed in the same way as the organization itself. Research into alliance capability has shown this notion to be false. Alliances require different tools and different attitudes.

Table 1. Tools for alliance management.

- Alliance training: attending alliance training is mainly useful to gret bacsic knowledge about structural, relational and legal aspects. It is relevant for people new to alliances.
- Evaluation: this is a particularly strong tool when alliances are not evaluated individually, but are compared to one another as well. Such evaluation stimulates the transfer of alliance knowledge inside the firm. Moreover, the inclusion of partners in the evaluation allows a firm to get a complete picture of alliance performance.
- Alliance specialist: having an alliance expert inside the firm is helpful, provided that such person is not to far removed from line management. Usually this specialist is responsible for finding best practices in alliance management, organizing alliance workshops and documenting and disseminating knowledge inside his firm.
- Database: access to experiences, tools checklists, and information about partners can support managers of alliances in their daily work.
- Partner programs: these programs allow firms to keep track of and coordinate a large number of partners. Firms like Oracle and Compaq provide access to (parts of) their partner program on their websites.
- Portfolio analysis: currently the most advanced tool in alliance management, portfolio analysis allows firms to optimize, not just individual alliances, but their entire alliance portfolio.

Source: Draulans, De Man and Volberda (1999), Duysters, De Man and Wildeman (1999), Harbison and Pekar (1997)

Competitive Advantage and Alliance Capability

Of course the interesting thing about alliance capabilities is not that they enhance a company's alliance performance, as such. The truly important element is that alliance capabilities play a role in the competitive process and can underpin a competitive advantage. From the perspective of competitive advantage, an alliance capability can perform three roles (see Table 2):

- Critical success factor. An alliance capability is a critical success factor when it contributes to alliance success, but when alliances themselves are not key to gaining a competitive advantage. Typical

Table 2. Alliance capability as a source of competitive advantage.

Alliance capability as a:	Charcteristic:	Example:
Critical success factor	Capability increases the success rate of alliances, but alliances are not critical for outperfoming competitors; it supports competitive advantage	Alliances aimed at optimization, efficiency, cost management
Core competence	Superior performance in alliances allows the firm to out perform its competitors; alliance capability is source of competitive advantage	Starbuck's Coffee, Nike
Qualifier	Ability to manage alliances successfully is a prerequisite for firm survival in its industry; absence of a capability is a severe competitive disadvantage	Car industry, Silicon Valley, airlines

examples include joint ventures aimed at reaping economies of scale in the chemical and oil industry. These are important in managing costs, but are more a tool to optimize than a powerful competitive weapon. Nonetheless, they require an alliance capability to make them work. In this role an alliance capability is of interest to the firms in the alliance, but has little consequences outside the alliance. It may support a competitive advantage, but is not its source.

- Core competence. When a firm is able to use alliances pro-actively for example for speeding up the innovation process or getting access to customers and technologies, a firm may outperform its competitors. If smart alliance management creates a distinctive competitive position, the alliance capability has become a core competence: a source of competitive advantage. Firms with such a superior skill in alliance management include Starbuck's Coffee and Nike.

- Qualifier. In many industries nowadays, allying and networking has become so pervasive that it is virtually impossible to operate successfully without alliances (and as a consequence without an alliance capability). These industries include the car industry (with its supplier networks), many high tech sectors (in Silicon Valley survival is impossible without inter-firm cooperation) and the airline industry (in which several major alliance groups compete head on). When alliance capability has become a prerequisite for survival, it has become a qualifier, meaning that in order to qualify at all for a position in that industry, a firm must have an alliance capability. Not possessing one puts a firm at a severe disadvantage.

The Future of Alliance Capability

In the 1970s, alliance capabilities mainly performed the role of critical success factor. In the course of the 1980s various firms started to develop their alliance capability into a core competence. In the 1990s, with the advent of the network economy, alliance capability is becoming a qualifier in an increasing amount of industries. Of course some industries (like the car industry and the high tech industry) are ahead in this development, while others (especially the service industry and agriculture) appear to trail somewhat behind. However with the increasing amount of alliances being formed in all sectors of economic activity, it can be expected that alliance capability will become a qualifier in a rising number of industries. The demands made by competition on a firm's alliance performance push alliance capability from being a critical success factor towards being a core competence and next, in the direction of a qualifier.

If this indeed happens, then no firm will be able to survive without an alliance capability. Those firms who are still seeing an alliance capability as a critical success factor may underestimate its importance and will need to give more attention to learning about alliances. Those firms seeing alliance capability as a core competence, need to be aware of the possibility that sooner or later the advantage of this core competence will be eroded, when other firms build up a similar alliance capability. Finally, in those industries where alliance capability is a qualifier, firms should continually monitor the capability and be on the lookout for new alliance management knowledge. They are to avoid being overtaken by new developments in the rapidly expanding field of alliance management and should take care not to be put at a competitive disadvantage from which they cannot recover. Benchmarking alliance performance, followed by implementation of best practices is a prerequisite in this phase.

Summary

An important cause of the low success rates of alliances is that many firms do not possess an alliance capability. An alliance capability consists of the alliance experience of a firm and the alliance tools it has implemented to manage its alliances. In some industries, alliance capability is a core competence: firms can create a distinctive position vis-à-vis competitors by smart alliance management. In an increasing number of industries, however, an alliance capability becomes a prerequisite for survival. In these industries, firms will be at a competitive *dis*advantage when they do not master the art of alliance management.

References

Booz Allen & Hamilton, 1997, *Cross-Border Alliances in the Age of Collaboration*, Los Angeles, Booz Allen & Hamilton.

Booz Allen & Hamilton, 1998, *Institutionalizing Alliance Skills: Secrets of Repeatable Success*, Los Angeles, Booz Allen & Hamilton.

Draulans, J., A.-P. de Man and H.W. Volberda, 1999, and "Alliantievaardigheid: een bron van concurrentievoordeel", *Holland/Belgium Management Review*, No. 63, January, pp. 52–59.

Duysters, G., A.-P. de Man and L. Wildeman, 1999, "A network approach to alliance management", *European Management Journal*, Vol. 17, No. 2, pp. 182–187.

Gulati, R., 1999, "Network location and learning: the influence of network resources and firm capabilities on alliance formation", *Strategic Management Journal*, vol. 20, no. 5, pp. 397–420

Harbison, J. and P. Pekar, 1997, *A Practical Guide to Alliances: Leapfrogging the Learning Curve*, Booz Allen & Hamilton.

KPMG, 1996, *Alliances and Networks: The Next Generation*, KPMG, Amsterdam.

Chapter 8

A Dancing Elephant Is Still an Elephant: The Challenges Facing Multinationals Working in Alliance-Mode

Joan E. van Aken

L14
L24
F23

Alliances with independent partners are becoming increasingly important if Multinational Enterprises (MNEs) are to compete in an ever more rapidly changing and competitive environment. "Nobody can do it alone anymore" (J.R. Houghton of Corning Glass, Business Week, 1993). This not only applies to Small and Medium Sized Enterprises (SMEs) with their relatively limited resources and capabilities, but to Multinational Enterprises (MNEs) as well.

The basic strategic reasons for the increased importance of alliances, i.e. close collaboration between independent partners, are well known (see e.g. Doz and Hamel, 1998). They stem from increased competitive pressures (hyper-competition, globalization, rapid technological developments) in combination with increasingly efficient industrial markets (among others through TQM and ICT). These factors both force and enable companies to concentrate on a few core capabilities, which are — and can remain — of world class level and to subcontract or outsource almost all other inputs to their business. Subsequently, in order to safeguard the uninterrupted supply and the sustained adaptation of strategic inputs to their needs, companies forge strong relations with the suppliers of these strategic inputs.

MNEs often prefer to work in stand-alone mode as long as all the required capabilities are in-house and of competitive standard. In an increasing number of cases, however, this no longer holds and the switch is made to working in alliance-mode, i.e. operating a business by combining the resources and capabilities of independent partners. Working in full alliance-mode may not only mean engaging in one or a few major alliances, it may mean a whole portfolio of alliances. It may also involve close collaboration with suppliers of key parts or it may even mean having personnel of independent partners operating like one's own personnel (like when outsourcing essential IT-functions, or like the Brazilian Volkswagen factory, where the personnel of independent suppliers mount their parts on Volkswagen cars, themselves).

In an influential book Kanter (1990) called for MNEs to become much more flexible. According to her simile, the elephants should learn to dance, alone, but also with partners. I argue that a dancing elephant is still an elephant. Should a MNE want to operate in full alliance-mode, it should not try to learn to dance, instead it should transform itself into a pack of hunting wolves.

Problems of the Alliance Mode

Working in alliance-mode is not without its problems, however. The reason is twofold. Firstly, in stand-alone mode managing for business results is strongly supported by the "classical trinity" of unity of ownership, power and loyalty. In alliance-mode, on the other hand, one has to manage under conditions of distributed ownership, power and loyalty (Van Aken, Hop and Post, 1998). Distributed ownership can lead to conflicts of interest. Distributed power means that instead of depending on hierarchy, one has to reach consensus with one's partners when it comes to solving conflicts and the creation of strategic direction for the collaboration. In addition, the people involved are usually more loyal to their own company than they are to the combination.

Secondly, alliances often have the liability of newness (Hannan and Freeman, 1989): the relevant business formula is still to be developed and, as yet, the partners lack a common "relational infrastructure" which supports communication, understanding, trust and decision-making. Therefore, alliances have a failure rate of somewhere between that of start-up companies and well-established companies (see e.g. studies by McKinsey and Coopers & Lybrand, cited in Business Week, July 21, 1986).

Design or Learn

In order to improve the success rate of alliances, many authors advocate a kind of design-approach (see e.g. Harbison and Pekar, 1998): invest more effort in analysis of context, strategy and possible partners, in the subsequent design of the alliance agreement and in the set-up of the collaboration (an aspect often heavily supported by legal and financial experts). It is seldom a bad idea to look before you leap, but usually this will only solve one's problem in situations of "near-equilibrium" (Stacey, 1995), i.e. if one intends to create a new situation which is close to the ones one knows. In the formation of alliances this is often not the case. Adopting a learning-approach may then be a better idea.

Good examples of applying a learning-approach to alliance-formation and alliance-operation can be found in SMEs working in alliance-mode in productive clusters or industrial districts (see e.g. Porter, 1998). In such cases, SMEs operate by using flexible combinations of capabilities of various independent partners. In productive industrial districts this is done on the basis of a well-developed alliance-infrastructure, i.e. a network of social and business relations between individuals, groups and organisations in which a company is embedded (Gulati, 1998). Such networks of relations develop on the basis of purely social interactions, including family ties, and the social interactions accompanying business transactions. Furthermore, they are strongly supported by spatial and cultural proximity. Entrepreneurs tend to invest heavily in such social networks. These informal social and business networks form the breeding ground for the formation of a large variety of alliances. Usually such alliances are emergent, i.e. they are not formalised from the beginning, but emerge from initially satisfying business transactions. Further development of the alliance — or the dissolution of the alliance — is based on the increasing (or decreasing) mutual trust in the integrity and professional competence between the partners and in the viability of the common venture. A similar learning-approach is used for structuring the alliance, i.e. the allocation of resources to the common venture, the division of tasks among the partners and the definition and assignment of managerial tasks. Structuring is driven by problem solving and based on experimentation and learning, rather than on a pre-defined design.

In the learning-approach described above, the difficulties of working in alliance-mode — absence of the classical trinity and the liability of newness — are overcome by various mechanisms. Emerging collaboration on the basis of increasing mutual trust among the partners and in the common venture may overcome the problems of distributed ownership and power: initial investments are limited so that ownership issues are relatively unimportant and the increasing trust supports the development of consensus.

The strong, pre-existing social relations in combination with cultural and spatial proximity can overcome the problems of distributed loyalty. It also supports the development towards consensus and thus lightens the problems of distributed power. In addition, a learning-approach can overcome the problems due to the liability of newness.

How Alliances Challenge MNE's

MNEs may want to emulate such a learning-approach to working in alliance-mode. However, there are important differences between SMEs and MNEs in their approaches to alliances. The MNE-approach is characterized by:

- alliance-formation by professional, hierarchically organised management instead of by owner-entrepreneurs;

- formal organisation of the "fuzzy-front-end" of the collaboration by elaborate collaboration agreements, instead of a learning-approach;
- a (large) portfolio of important as well as less-important alliances, often with the same (large) partner, instead of one or just a few key alliances;
- more organisational inertia: learning to work in alliance-mode is also an issue of organisational change, and large organisations tend to be more difficult to change than smaller ones;
- a tendency to regard an alliance as a profitable contract, still a kind of business transaction, as opposed to a productive collaboration that has to be managed and continually adapted to new developments;
- a tendency of promising early contacts between senior managers of potential partners, based on win-win expectations, swamped by the subsequent efforts of legal and accounting specialists who fear lose-win results;
- a quest for control, and hence a tendency to prefer take-overs above alliances with their accompanying management problems of the missing classical trinity.

A final difference between SMEs operating in productive industrial districts and MNEs, is that the former use their cultural and spatial proximity to overcome some of the problems of working in full alliance-mode, while alliances among MNEs usually also have to overcome the problems of bridging cultural and spatial divides. However, a key asset of successful MNEs is their competence in doing just that.

Implementing Alliances in MNEs

First of all, the application by MNEs of the learning approach to working in alliance-mode involves the creation of a fertile alliance-infrastructure. This is achieved by investing time and management attention in business and social relations with potential partners and by initiating many, possibly informal, small-scale collaborative ventures (several of which may be undertaken merely to test the integrity and competence of potential partners for more ambitious ventures). In this way a great many options for productive alliances are created. In case one wants to call one of those options, the start would be small-scale and informal, so one can gradually develop the business formula for the venture and also the appropriate structure for the alliance. At a later stage, formalisation will just be a matter of confirming existing agreements and working arrangements, based on existing mutual trust (as opposed to a design-approach, where the bargaining about the alliance contract is used as a mechanism to hammer out the various aspects of the collaboration).

In such an approach it is useful to distinguish between alliance-governance — management charged with the formation of a certain alliance and its strategic management — and the operational management of that alliance, and separate the two. At alliance-governance level one has to deal with partner selection and the definition of the strategic direction and the overall structure of the collaborative venture, thus dealing with the problems of distributed ownership and power. Once these issues have been adequately solved, operational management is allocated the necessary resources needed for the venture and it can manage these resources under conditions of quasi-unity of ownership and power. It should then be able to deal with the problems of distributed loyalty. The problems of the liability of newness are dealt with in the manner described, i.e. by starting the venture with small-scale experimentation on the basis of a pre-existing relational infrastructure.

This approach is infeasible in a monolithically organised MNE, where alliance-formation is the sole prerogative of senior management: one has to be "internally networked" in order to be able to work in full alliance-mode, externally. Otherwise, the potential partners always have to deal with the company-as-a-whole instead of with an agile part of it. The natural flow of events in alliance-formation is frustrated if, for key decisions, one has to escalate to senior management every time, while senior management, meanwhile, gets overloaded. Besides, senior management simply lacks the time to invest in the creation of an alliance-infrastructure, apart from relations with a few big partners. Thus, in order to operate in full alliance-mode, it is advantageous for a

MNE to be organised as a system of semi-autonomous businesses, with a management empowered to conclude alliances. In other words, to be organised along the lines of a pack of hunting wolves, rather than trying to become an agile elephant.

A design-approach to alliance-formation can be quite productive if the potential partners are already well known and well connected to each other and if the potential venture has little secrets for its partners. Otherwise, a learning approach is advisable.

A learning approach also has its limitations, of course. Big deals with big partners will still require heavy involvement of senior management. And semi-autonomous businesses may still have many mutual interdependencies (like, perhaps, common local sales organisations), which may be influenced by alliances and thus need coordination. Furthermore, MNEs often use a fair degree of formalisation of their management systems to overcome the problems concerning their size and the cultural and spatial divides among their units, thus restricting the flexible adaptation of these systems to the needs of new alliances. Nevertheless, the opportunities of the increasingly interconnected business world and of the flexible combination of resources and capabilities of world-class partners are such that in many industries corporate elephants are becoming an endangered species, even if they have learnt to dance. Packs of wolves have the future.

References

Doz, Y.L. and G. Hamel, 1998, *Alliance Advantage*, Boston: Harvard Business School Press.

Gulati, R. 1998, "Alliances and networks", *Strategic Management Journal* 1998, pp. 293–317.

Hannan, M.T. and J. Freeman, 1989, *Organizational Ecology*, Boston: Harvard Business School Press.

Kanter, R.M., 1990, *When Giants Learn to Dance: Mastering the Challenge of Strategy, Management and Careers in the 1990's*, New York: Simon and Schuster.

Porter, M. 1998, "Clusters and the new economies of competition", *Harvard Business Review* (November–December) pp. 77–90.

Stacey, R.D. 1995, "The science of complexity. An alternative perspective for strategic change processes", *Strategic Management Journal* 16, pp. 477–495.

Van Aken, J.E., L. Hop and G. Post, 1998, "The virtual organization: a special mode of strong inter-organizational cooperation" in Hitt, M.A., J.E. Ricart and R.D. Nixon: *Managing Strategically in an Interconnected World*, Chicester: Wiley, pp. 301–320.

Chapter 9

Four Critical Skills for Managing High Performance Alliances

Robert Porter Lynch

L14
L24

While most companies have come to recognize the tremendous value an alliance may bring, senior executives all-too-often fail to see that value materialize because of ineffective skills in alliance management. Typically the business development and legal team that formed the alliance has jumped to their next deal. The alliance is never placed on an organization chart thereby gaining little attention from senior management, and the human resource department has no idea of the critical factors for success in assigning the right people.

Facing the Alliance Management Problem

Placing too little effort on managing alliances results in comments like these:

"We know how to create alliances, but don't know how to manage them!" reflected one American top executive, who lamented the lack of success in achieving his alliance's primary goals.

"It looked great on paper, but it was a terrible fit in reality. Our cultures clashed on every issue from decision making processes to rewarding our sales force." stated a dejected alliance manager in the pharmaceutical industry.

"During negotiations, the deal makers poisoned the well, and we haven't yet recovered. We had to undo all the damage caused by the

adversary legal jargon." was the battle-weary response of the president of a multi-billion dollar international joint venture.

"Alliances are an unnatural act for us. They are extremely difficult to manage; we'd prefer to do acquisitions." complained a senior vice president of a large German chemical manufacturer. Later, he noted that 30% of his revenues and nearly 50% of his division's profits came from alliances, but *"we spend only 5% of our management time on them."* For some inexplicable reason he failed to allocate management resources to the highest profit generator in his business.

These types of comments are all-too-common. Each executive fell into the alliance management trap. None of the executives had considered the fact that alliances must be managed, and that the most critical management issues should be an integral part of the negotiations.

Alliances are a very different form of business genre than managing an internal business unit. Fundamentally, executives who have been managing in traditional hierarchical command and control companies are befuddled when given an alliance assignment. The synergy they seek from the alliance remains elusive; cultural differences become insurmountable obstacles; project management turns into problem management; and the bureaucracies of the two parent organizations become a quagmire of politics.

However, not every alliance must face such impasses.

"I am amazed how well our two companies are working together. We are actually ahead of schedule, and have had relatively few difficulties;" was the delighted comment from the alliance manager of a strategic sourcing venture composed of European food service company with an American partner.

"After only six weeks of working together, it's hard to tell the difference between the employees of their company and ours;" explained the director of an international mining company, commenting about his alliance with an electronics firm.

These alliance managers achieved success because they insisted their joint teams spend ample time understanding the unique aspects of alliances, building cross-cultural teamwork, and establishing processes and skills to access the unique value of an alliance.

Our experience has shown that there are four critical skills, which are often overlooked, that enable alliance managers to produce high performance results: skills at managing differences, breakthroughs, speed, and transformation.

Skill in Managing Differences

The fundamental reason why alliances are formed is to access a capability within another company, thus finding the magical synergy, the 1+1=3 potential. However, this means capturing the value of differences.

Lying within the inherent capability differences is the promise of the alliance to create bold new futures, or conversely, to implode upon itself. These cultural differences are derived not just from ethnic and national sources, but also from corporate and industry cultures. As more and more companies globalize and form cross-industry alliances, being able to capitalize upon cultural differences, and avoid cross-cultural implosion, will become a critical competitive advantage.

Traditional approaches to managing cultural differences have focused on becoming sensitive to differences, cross-cultural training, understanding linguistic nuances, and acculturation. While these methods have their worth, we have found three very essential elements are often overlooked.

First: *The Power of Vision.* The universal vitality of focusing on a powerful common vision, backed up by a dynamic and inspiring value proposition that speaks to the customer shows no cultural boundaries. For example, take this typical vision for alliances: *"We will be the leaders in our industry."* It presents a "vision vacuum" by saying nothing, containing no commitments, and inspiring neither the alliance partners nor the customers. Devoid of a powerful vision, everything defaults to politics, manifesting as cultural differences, which then divide the alliance partners against themselves. As the old adage from Alice in Wonderland states: "if you don't know where you are going, any road will get you there." And that road will be fraught with in fighting, subversion, despair, and confusion, all of which will ultimately lead to the ruin of the alliance.

Contrast the weakness of a faulty vision with the motivational force of a more commanding perspective: "*Our alliance will create 10 new innovations each year that will reduce the costs to our customers by 25%, while accelerating their throughput by 50%.*" By having a powerful central vision, alliance partners focus differences on how to achieve the joint goal, rather than arguing amongst themselves as to whose way is the "right way."

Powerful visions are all founded on belief in the ability to discover the unknown, accomplish the seemingly impossible, and overcome the apparently unattainable. Therefore, strong alliance leadership must be present to build such a vision and to unify and align the alliance's differences for a common purpose.

Second: *The Synergy of Compatible Differences.* Synergy does not just occur as a natural byproduct of alliance formation. Rather, it must be designed with architectural aplomb. But more, synergy must be activated by a powerful set of actions founded upon the understanding of how differentials produce the 1+1=3 effect.

"*If two people in the same room think alike, one is unnecessary,*" the philosopher Ernest Holmes. The eminent psychologist, Carl Gustav Jung foresaw the potential of alliances when he said: "*The greater the contrast, the greater the potential. Great energy only comes from a correspondingly great tension between opposites.*" Joel Barker, in his groundbreaking work on paradigms recognized that new paradigms originate from outsiders who think differently, not from insiders who see their world from an old and tired perspective. Each of these men understood the profound impact differences can have on the co-creation of bold new futures.

Invariably, however, ethnocentrism attempts to enforce its mighty hand. Some members of the alliance begin making judgments regarding the other side's culture, branding it as strange, wrong, inefficient, bad, or unproductive. As soon as this begins, fear, uncertainty, doubt, and distrust begin to fester, and then the alliance begins to unravel. This calls for strong action.

Adept alliance managers, leveraging the vision for the alliance, will call for creating a "synergy of compatible differences" in which differences are respected as source of innovation, cherished for their ability to break paradigms, and expected to produce creative solutions. The manager's ability to create this new "super-ordinate" culture within the alliance enables the alliance to produce at higher performance levels than either parent company can achieve.

Third: *Highly Differentiated Alliances Require Integrators.* Not every successful line manager makes a great alliance manager. Because alliances cannot be commanded, the mechanisms for leadership and control are dramatically different compared with most conventional organizations. Great alliance managers tend to be "integrators," possessing outstanding skills in bridging differences through their ability to translate across cultural boundaries. The greater the differential between cultures, the greater the need for highly skilled integrators.

For example, in a genomics alliance, bio-technologists will be neither versed in the intricacies of computer database analysis nor will information systems specialists understand the complexities of cellular biology. This alliance requires an integrator who understands both biology and computers to connect across the cultural divide.

Good integrators usually have had zigzag careers. Perhaps they've held a technology degree, but spent extensive time in marketing and sales. Integrators are often exceptional coordinators. Yet their bridge building often looks invisible to outsiders, and thus is seldom rewarded.

Often the effective integrator will develop principles and values for the alliance that forge unity of vision and purpose. Integrators know "people support what they help create." Thus, they use techniques is to ask unifying questions that draw out the answers from their teams.

Whenever conflict arises (and it will, for wherever there is change, their will be conflict) the integrator is careful to focus conflict on ideas and issues, steering clear of ego entrapment games, such as "who's right or wrong," or "what's good or bad."

Skill at managing diversity of thinking is a fundamental underpinning in the next skill-set, because paradigm shifting is essential to all breakthrough innovation.

Skill in Managing Breakthroughs

Once the foundation is laid for managing differences, then the alliance is poised to design and create breakthroughs. What many don't realize is that breakthrough innovation, more often than not, actually come through design, not chance. In fact, today 40% of all breakthrough technology is now being developed through alliances.

The originator of breakthrough design was Thomas Edison, the holder of over 1000 patents. When he established his first laboratory in 1872, it was staffed by a team of a dozen diverse technical specialists — a mechanic, a chemist, a glass blower, and a machinist, among others. Edison, carrying his small notebook everywhere, would give assignments to his teams, and, as they worked, he would circulate among them, asking questions, taking in information, making notes, assimilating ideas. All this time, he was co-creating with his team. Using his power of inquiry, Edison was able to pose questions that stretched the minds of his team. Then, taking their highly diverse inputs, ideas, and perspectives, Edison would craft the next phase of the experiment, until he was able to make the invention emerge from the great confluence of all their collective ideas.

The first step in launching a breakthrough project is to declare a breakthrough goal. For example, upon opening his laboratory, Edison announced: *"We will create one minor invention every ten days, and one major invention every six weeks."* Similarly, 100 years later Gordon Moore at Intel proclaimed: *"The speed of a computer chip will double every 18 months, and the cost per byte will be cut in half."* A breakthrough declaration derives its power by aligning people's minds in the same direction, by creating a quantum jump objective; by making the goal highly measurable; thus motivating the mind to action.

Next, alliance managers will also make it possible for breakdowns to become the source of creative energy. While it may surprise many, high performance teams actually have more breakdowns than low performance teams. The difference is how breakdowns are handled. Effective alliance managers energize creative forces by focusing on how to turn breakdowns into breakthroughs, by seeking hidden meaning, and expanding learning by asking lots of questions, such as "What's missing?" "What's possible?" "What shifts in thinking are required?" They focus on team responsibility, not the individual. Blame is seldom, if ever, used as a management technique. Creative "dissidents" are often members of breakthrough teams because their ideas keep the breakthrough teams on its toes. The alliance's corporate sponsors support the use of breakthrough teams by avoiding too much bureaucracy and slowness of decision making, seeing see the alliance as a laboratory of experimental change.

Setting the stage for a Breakthrough Project requires that certain conditions be present. Something must trigger action — there must be some breakdowns or conditions of stress present. For example: "customers are complaining," "competitors are devouring our market share," or "our products are malfunctioning." Then top management must demand extraordinary action: "our survival is a stake," "we must take emergency action," "time is running out," "you have only three months to design and implement a program."

Once triggering conditions in place, alliance managers will establish a Breakthrough Project Team comprised of members with diversity of input and viewpoint that are to confront traditional paradigms. They must have a propensity to diagnose problems and seek new patterns, while making a powerful commitment to the project, with a clear vision of what is possible, and a real belief that new levels of achievement are possible.

The Breakthrough Team will first focus on an achieving a short-term performance breakthrough aimed at getting quick results, thus building trust, confidence, and strategic momentum for the long term goal. Don't throw lots of money at such a team, minimal additional resources actually forces greater creativity. The idea is to *produce better results with the same resources.*

Breakthroughs are beyond what is predictable. Breakthrough Teams all comment that they may not know how to attain a breakthrough when they start, but the very process of committing to a breakthrough tends to make unique things happen. All sorts of creative forces come to play.

Skill in Managing Speed of Decision Making

One of the most dramatic business changes in the last decade has been the unprecedented shift in the "clock speed"– the underlying velocity at which decisions and change has accelerated. As one alliance manager humorously commented: *"One day my boss asked me to submit a status report to him concerning a project I was working on. I asked him if tomorrow would be soon enough. He said, 'If I wanted it tomorrow, I would have waited until tomorrow to ask for it!'"*

This almost shocking rate of change and speed in the business environment has had massive implications on the way alliances are being managed.

A slow moving world allowed decisions to be based on a linear progression of information. Where the future was more predictable and somewhat certain, after gathering information, the risk of most decisions could be analysed, discount factors could be applied to financial evaluations, and corporations, in their ponderous way, would move forward with their strategic plans marked out in five-year increments. Slow-time managers wanted no surprises, with risk control reigning supreme.

However, everything has been altered in the fast-time world of the new millennium. The linear analytical skills necessary are no longer as useful, and in many cases are obsolete. No longer is it possible to base valid decisions on sufficiently good information, because, in today's fast-time world, the longer one takes to gather information, the more the world changes, and the less valid the information originally gathered. In other words, delay decision-making in the hope of gaining accuracy, the *more inaccurate* the information becomes and the *riskier* the decision. (See Figure 1.) Anyone expecting to gather facts to gain surety of their decision will always be too late to capture opportunities. Alliance managers who have worked in traditional, slow moving industries, such as paper and chemicals, have experienced this phenomenon when trying to negotiate with telecom and computer companies. While grinding out tedious five-year financial analyses, the traditional companies watched the business models of the fast companies' morph several times, often losing out to other faster, less risk-averse competitors. The skills that served the conservative planner in the slow-time world is nothing more than analysis paralysis in fast time.

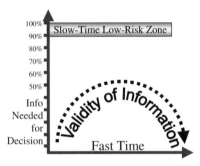

Figure 1. Information validity in a fast time world.

This fast-time phenomenon calls on alliance managers to develop and nurture a very different set of skills (many of which are not likely to be cherished in all but the most advanced companies). Some of these new alliance management skills include the ability to move adroitly in a highly unpredictable world, where there may be multiple alliances to handle multiple future scenarios, high tolerance for ambiguity and uncertainty, less analysis and more synthesis, and fundamentally more non-linear thinking.

In this fast-time environment, risk management must rely more on systems analysis, multiple and parallel options, and methods that enable flexible decision points and rapid redesign. (See Figure 2.) In an environment where multiple alliances will be used to hedge against multiple potential futures, instead of managing single alliances, as was the norm in the slow-time world, the alliance manager is faced with managing a large portfolio of alliances, often among competitors.

Lastly, in managing speed, corporate sponsors must be careful not to overlay both their management reporting systems on the alliance, thereby creating a dual reporting system for the alliance managers. What's more effective is to determine leading indicators of success,

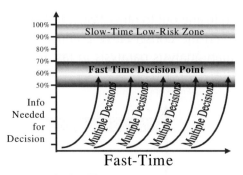

Figure 2. Multiple alliance decisions to hedge bets.

such as critical market impact factors, innovations created, more effective organizational resource utilization, or relative competitive advantage. In a world that's moving faster and faster all the time, it's undesirable to managing by lagging indicators, such as past financial performance.

Skill in Managing Transformation

A fast moving world causes the strategic driving forces that formed the essence of the alliance to be in a constant state of flux, serving as a major destabilizing factor, like a rogue wave trying to capsize a boat. Thus, alliances are in constant need of transformation. Alliance managers must be monitoring the shifts in the strategic environment regularly, and repositioning their parents and partners to align with the shifts.

One very valuable tool to track the fluctuating forces is value migration, which tracks how the essential ingredients of value to the customer change over time as new technologies change the rules of business, or as new competitors drive down profit margins, or fragmented solutions become more integrated. Figure 3 illustrates how IBM was faced with massive value migration shifts, which fundamentally changed the nature of its business and strategic alliances. Astute alliance managers are tuned to the leading indicators of these shifts, so that they can be proactive, rather than reactive, in responding to changes. As one manager of a ten-year old successful alliance in the chemicals industry

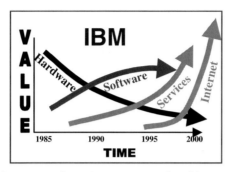

Figure 3. Value migration curve faced by IBM.

saw: "*Value migration is changing my entire alliance. We will be obsolete and competitively disadvantaged in a year unless we reconfigure the entire strategy and bring in new technology.*"

Developing a set of value migration curves for an alliance is more an art than a science, but it causes alliance partners to project the future, position resources, plan strategies, and respond to competitive incursions adroitly.

Because the alliance must transform itself frequently or lose its competitive edge, repeated renegotiation of strategic, financial, market, and operational interests should be expected. Therefore, alliance managers must establish a culture of visioning, breakthroughs, and co-creation as a foundation for their renegotiations. Negotiating styles that are overly legalistic, win-lose, or adversarial in any way will be highly detrimental to the overall health of the alliance in an environment of frequent repositioning. As one telecom executive said of his alliance in Poland: "*No one knows what the future will look like. But if we don't talk about it, we will end up someplace else.*"

The Alliance Advantage

Alliances, by their very nature, possess a unique "hidden asset" — diversity of viewpoint — which, for the most part, goes either *untapped* or is *seen as an obstacle.* However, in the high performance alliance, diversity is a unique opportunity to capitalize on breakthroughs. By investing in effective alliance management, this asset can become produce a long stream of innovation and competitive advantage.

Today, the rate of change in the business world is far faster than the speed at which the traditional organization adapts to change. Consequently, organizations that have mastered success in one era easily become burdened in the next era, as the ebb and flow of paradigm shifts hit at shorter and shorter intervals. For these companies, adeptness in the art of managing alliances enables the creation of bold new futures and rapid regeneration.

Chapter 10

Tech Alliances: Managing Your Alliance Portfolio

Bonnie Beerkens and Charmianne Lemmens

L14
L24

This article analyzes the different sorts of alliances firms have at their disposal in dealing with the turbulence of high technology sectors, further referred to as portfolio building blocks. Firms that have created the right mix of portfolio building blocks will be better able to meet the diverse demands of a high tech business environment. Two types of alliances are described; fruit fly alliances and elephant alliances. Also two types of relationships can be distinguished, i.e. strong and weak relationships. This paper shows that fruit fly alliances can be used in both strong and weak relationships. In weak relationships they are used as a scanning device, and may be referred to as option alliances. In a strong relationship, fruit fly alliances are referred to as project alliances, where partners cooperate in consecutive projects over a specific period of time. In this way, firms can form a strong relationship with companies in other technological clusters. Therefore, building a strong relationship with the help of fruit fly alliances is the way to be innovative while preserving trust. This form of cooperation is very useful in rapidly changing technological environments.

Introduction

In order to meet the competitive challenges in the rapidly evolving network economy, firms tend to rely more and more on knowledge alliances. The increase in the number of knowledge alliances has led to the emergence of complex inter-organizational networks in which firms are linked to each other either directly or indirectly. Alliances have developed from dyadic relations (see Figure 1(a)) in the post-industrial age into alliance networks (see Figure 1(b)) in the digital age (Vasudevan & Duysters, 1998). These days firms are actually caught in a web of relations. This has important consequences for alliance partners, because they have to be aware that their actions are influenced by the behavior of partner firms in their network. For knowledge acquisition these firms can rely on partners in their own web of relations, but they can also explore new combinations of knowledge and link up with

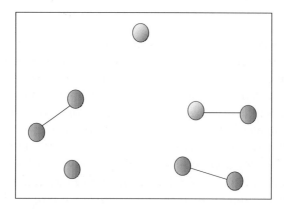

Figure 1(a). Dyadic ties.

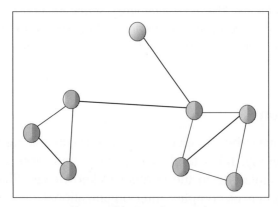

Figure 1(b). Social network.

other technological clusters in the network. Some advantages and disadvantages of being embedded in a network are listed in Table 1.

Table 1. Embeddedness.

Advantages of embeddedness:
• Firms that have strong relationships in a network have access to unique information about partners' capabilities, their reliability and the availability of possible partners in the network.
• The likelihood that a firm acts unethically is decreased when the firm is embedded in a network of relations, since this behavior is communicated quickly to other partners. Hence, the reputation of the opportunistic firm can be damaged.
• As a result of their embedded relations, firms with more social capital will not only have access to information about a larger number of alliances, but they may also be able to attract better partners who want to collaborate with them (Gulati, 1998).
Disadvantages of embeddedness:
• Relationships can be redundant to the extent that they indirectly lead to the same partners and thus provide the same information benefits.
• Partner firms in the network influence the firm's behavior.

In describing knowledge alliances, we take on a social network perspective, which describes alliance partners as firms, which are connected by either strong or weak ties (Granovetter, 1973). This approach is complemented by a managerial approach, which distinguishes different types of alliances. These are fruit flies and elephants, both metaphors for different types of alliances (Spekman & Lambe, 1997). In this paper we aim to combine those two perspectives, resulting in a managerial model of portfolio building blocks, that makes a distinction between alliance types (the managerial viewpoint) and types of relationships (the social network perspective). The distinction between types of relationships and alliances adds value because it allows managers to get a better insight in the management of their alliance portfolio.

As will now be shown, these two perspectives can be combined into three different kinds of alliances: the portfolio building blocks (see Figure 2).

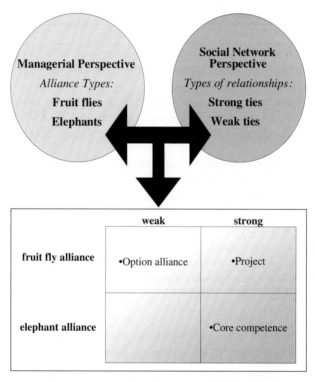

Figure 2. Perspectives combined into the managerial model of portfolio building blocks.

Types of Alliances: Fruit Flies vs. Elephants (Managerial Perspective)

Fruit fly alliances are short-term alliances, often formed between partners from different technological clusters. The purpose of those alliances is to aim at innovation by scanning the environment for new technologies and exploring new combinations of knowledge by tapping into other technological clusters through collaboration (Duysters, De Man, & Wildeman, 1999).

The environment where fruit fly alliances are especially valuable is in markets that are uncertain and change rapidly. The duration of cooperation is short, and hence there is no time to build trust. An advantage of this alliance type is that firms do not become overly dependent on the collaborating partner to continue business operations as the relationship dissolves. A disadvantage is that this alliance type is not suitable to build up trust, which is required for successful knowledge acquisition and internalization. Therefore, firms in fruit fly types of alliances can optimize their exploration process by either:

- Looking for a set of partners to cooperate with more often over time. Here partners approach each other for cooperation again and again in consecutive projects, which breeds a history of cooperation and trust over time, even though those alliances may be of short duration.
- Relying on industry culture for basic rules of behavior. In order to build the trust that is required for a first-time cooperation, firms can not rely on a history of cooperation. Instead, they have to rely on the existing rules and procedures of the industry culture for establishing the alliance.

Unlike fruit flies, elephant alliances have a long life span, in which trust develops over time. Interdependence between the partners is high and renews over time. The purpose of the alliance is often related closely to the core competencies of the company. Characteristic for elephant alliances is that they learn through exploitation of existing knowledge and competencies. This in contrast to fruit fly alliances which aim at innovation. Therefore, elephant alliances are effective in more stable, predictable markets.

Whether firms are involved in fruit fly or elephant alliances, or both, does not tell a lot about the relationship underlying these forms of cooperation. This especially becomes clear if we take fruit fly alliances as an example. Fruit fly alliances can either exist in a weak or a strong type of relationship. A fruit fly alliance in a weak relationship can for instance be a first-time occasion, where the partners hardly know each other and where mutual trust is based on industry culture. In addition, a fruit fly alliance can be based on a shared history of consecutive cooperation, which represents a solid relationship. Thus, although both alliance types have an exploring character, they differ in the strength of the relationship. Hence, we should not only distinguish different types of alliances, but also types of relationships: strong and weak.

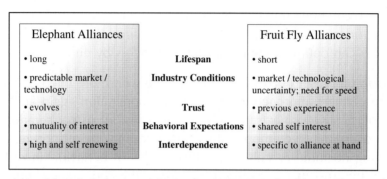

Source: Adapted from R. Spekman and C.J. Lambe, 1997, "Fruit Fly Alliances: The rise of Short-Lived Partnerships", The Alliance Analyst, August 15th 1997

Figure 3. Alliance comparison.

Types of Relationships: Strong and Weak Ties (Social Network Perspective)

Granovetter (1973) distinguishes relationships between actors into strong and weak ties. Strong and weak ties mainly differ from each other in the frequency of interaction between the partners in the relationship. Next to this, frequency of interaction, reciprocity, emotional intensity in the relationship, and intimacy (mutual confiding) between the actors (Brass, Butterfield, & Skaggs, 1998; Granovetter, 1973), determine whether there is a strong or weak tie (see Table 2).

The term "weak tie" describes the kind of relationship that can be characterized by infrequent interaction. Infrequent interaction implies there is little opportunity to build trust. Hence weak ties are often

Table 2. Characteristics of strong versus weak ties.

	Strong tie	Weak tie
Interaction	Frequent	Infrequent
Reciprocity	Yes	No
Emotional intensity	High	Low
Intimacy	High	Low
Commitment	High	Low
Risk arising from the opportunity to act unethical	High	Low
Risk arising from the likehood of unethical behavior	Low	High

considered to exist in a situation with little trust between the partners. In general, firms do not commit heavily to weak ties because there is low emotional intensity and intimacy between the partners. Weak ties are often considered to involve little risk, because there is only little opportunity to behave unethically since "individuals typically do not trust strangers with sensitive information" (Brass et al., 1998). Also, for the firm acting unethically, the sunk costs of investing in this social relationship are low, since there is low commitment (Brass et al., 1998). However, even though the *opportunity* for unethical behavior is small, the *likelihood* of unethical behavior is increased in weak relationships. Then, weak ties often bridge technological clusters. This implies that the partner in such a weak tie is not embedded in the direct network of the focal firm. Thus the partner in a weak tie usually is not connected, neither directly nor indirectly, to other partners of the focal firm. If one of the partners behaves unethically, this is not communicated to the rest of the network of this player (Brass et al., 1998). Hence, it is less likely that the reputation of the opportunistic actor will be damaged. And since the consequence of acting unethically, namely losing this very weak relationship, is not considerable, the likelihood of unethical behavior is increased. In this sense weak ties involve high risk.

Strong ties, on the other hand, are characterized by a solid, reciprocal and trustworthy relationship. The ties are strong, since there is frequent interaction and partners commit heavily to the relationship. This creates a large basis of trust and intimacy between the partners (Brass *et al.*, 1998; Granovetter, 1973). The opportunity for unethical behavior is clearly present, since partners in a strong relationship have to exchange sensitive information. Strong ties are therefore often considered to involve high risk. However, strong relationships are often embedded in a dense network, in which unethical behavior of actors is communicated quickly. As a consequence, their reputation can easily be damaged. Hence, the likelihood of unethical behavior is smaller than in the case of weak relationships. In this sense strong ties involve low risk.

The Social Network and Managerial Perspective Combined: The Model

The distinction between relationships into weak and strong and the distinction between fruit fly and elephant alliances leads, if combined, to a more complete model of different portfolio building blocks (see Figure 2):

- Option alliances
- Project alliances
- Core competence alliances

Option Alliances

Option alliances are fruit fly alliances, because there is relatively low commitment and the alliances are of relative short duration. The underlying relationship is weak because of the low basis of trust and the infrequency of interaction. This portfolio building block is used to scan the environment for new and potentially important technologies, and is often termed an option alliance. These alliances enable the focal firm to hedge against unforeseen technological changes in the industry, because they can be used to learn quickly about new technologies. If a technology proves to be worthwhile to invest in, the focal firm can use the acquired knowledge, without having to start from scratch with research. In this way firms do not have to invest heavily in every direction of technological change, which can later appear to be dead ends (Gomes-Casseres, 1996). Especially firms aiming at technological leadership in the industry rely on option alliances to stay ahead of competition with regard to innovations.

Option alliances typically concern collaborations between firms in different technological clusters. Hence cooperation may lead to more radical innovation than can ever be reached when only relying on partners within the focal firm's cluster. An example of an option alliance is Microsoft's big bet on 'WebTV.' Here Microsoft counts on innovative developments in the industry, which result in the usage of the TV as a PC. For this reason Microsoft acquired WebTV, in case the TV as a PC becomes the prevalent technology. However, apart from this big bet, Microsoft hedges the risk that not the technologies for WebTV, but the technologies that make the PC function as a television become the industry standard. This hedge is its DTV joint venture with Compaq and Intel. The goal of this joint venture is the development of comparative technologies to WebTV. Therefore the latter alliance can be regarded an option alliance.

Project Alliances

Project alliances occur when partners approach each other for consecutive cooperation. This situation is ideal in fast changing markets where rapid innovation is necessary to survive. In such a situation, projects evolve and dissolve in a relatively limited amount of time, and finding new partners time and time again is difficult. By cooperating repeatedly with the same partner, a strong relationship is built, while the alliances keep their flexibility. Hence a focal firm can gather a set of partners with whom a strong relationship is developed. These partners can be approached if their assistance in a project is needed.

The power of project alliances lies in the fact that trust has been built up as a result of a history of cooperation instead of similarity. Then, partners come from different technological clusters and thus have different technological knowledge and thinking patterns.

The case of IBM and Toshiba illustrates shared innovation through successive collaborations in the 1980s. With sales of $52 billion in 1986, IBM was still the world's largest computer maker, but it was not dominant in the microcomputer segment. It lacked amongst others the resources to develop the color flat-panel display technology in time, which was crucial for success in this market. Toshiba found itself in the same situation. By May 1988, the two companies first collaborated in a joint R&D project to develop new display technologies. This resulted in the development of the most advanced screen in the industry at that time. The joint R&D program was terminated after having reached this goal. A few months later they invested jointly in manufacturing facilities to produce a second generation of the screens by setting up a 50/50 joint venture headquartered in Japan: Display Technology Incorporated (DTI).

Core Competence Alliances

Core competence alliances occur in a strong relationship where the purpose of the alliance lies close to the core competencies of the partners. By seeking complementary capabilities through cooperation, the partners can strengthen their internal capabilities, which are crucial to their core competence.

An example of a core competence alliance is Goodyear; the world's leading tire company, and Michelin, another big player in the tire-industry, which announced a historical alliance in June 2000. The companies have been competing in the tire industry forever, now they agreed to jointly invest in the R&D of advanced run-flat technologies through a joint venture. Each company brings advanced run-flat system experience to the joint venture. Goodyear will license its extended mobility technology and pressure monitoring system patents to Michelin. Michelin will license the PAX System to Goodyear. Together Goodyear and Michelin decided the PAX system is the best platform from which to build new tire concepts. Obviously, the companies mutually exchange capabilities, which strengthen their core competence.

If firms compose an alliance portfolio involving these three portfolio building blocks, these firms can scan the business environment for promising new technologies by using option alliances, learn and experiment by using project alliances and strengthen core competencies by using competence alliances. Of course these relationships and portfolio building blocks are not static. It is key to portfolio thinking, to understand that these building blocks in the portfolio can evolve into each other, if the business environment requires such a move (see Figure 4). This should actually be a consciously chosen path.

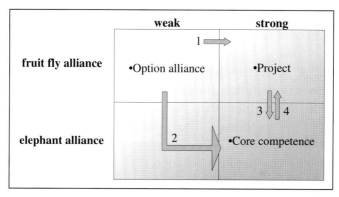

Figure 4. Transformation-cycle of portfolio building blocks.

Transformation-cycle of Network Building Blocks

1. *An option alliance can serve as a stepping stone to build a strong relationship and become a project alliance;* the strong relationship underlying the project alliance may evolve from an option alliance. If cooperation in the option alliance proves to be successful, the partners may decide to approach each other again if a new project comes up. This repeated cooperation strengthens the relationship, until it can be labeled a strong tie. Thus the transformation into a strong relationship implies that the option alliance, intended as a scanning device, now has the characteristics of a project alliance.

2. *An option alliance can at first maintain its weak character by transforming into an elephant alliance in a weak relationship, which serves as a stepping stone to a strong relationship and develop into a core competence alliance;* the step leading from fruit fly alliance in a weak relationship to an elephant alliance in a weak relationship seems unlikely. The question is whether it is possible for partners who just got acquainted to open up and enter into an alliance where the content is closely related to the partners' core competencies. The difficulty lies in the fact that trust is needed if partners have to reveal information on their competencies. Obviously, partners only do this to create a stronger relationship. Thus an elephant alliance in a weak relationship can only exist if it is a stepping stone to a strong relationship, i.e. a core competence alliance.

3. *A project alliance can retain its strong relationship and transform into a core competence alliance;* after cooperating on project base for a while, the partners may decide to enter into an alliance closer to the core competencies. Thus, these partners get involved in an elephant alliance with an underlying strong relationship, in other words, a core competence alliance.

4. *A core competence alliance can keep its strong character and transform into a project alliance;* if partners decide, after close cooperation in a core competence alliance, that the added value of such an intimate relationship is no longer significant, the partners may decide to resolve the core competence alliance and continue to cooperate on project base. This does not have to harm the underlying strong relationship if the partners agree on taking this step.

An example of this transformation cycle can clearly be found in Cargill Dow Polymers (CDP), which is a 50/50 joint venture between Cargill Incorporated and The Dow Chemical Corporation and which is the result of successive cooperation. The story starts with an option alliance, a 15-month joint development program during which Cargill and Dow Chemical combined their efforts to evaluate the potential for PLA polymers as well as the benefits of jointly pursuing PLA product development and marketing. PLA polymers can be used to make amongst others plastics and make up an entirely new product family as the first polymers to be derived from agricultural resources, such as corn. In November 1997 the success of this option alliance was followed by a project alliance, a 50/50 limited liability company, named Cargill Dow Polymers LLC, to develop and market polylactic acid (PLA). Cargill brought in process technology, low cost manufacturing and a strong patent portfolio of critical technology, while Dow's world class polymer science, applications technology and access to a global customer base should lead to the LLC's success. Again this cooperation proved to be successful. January 2000 Cargill Dow Polymers, an elephant alliance, was formed offering a resin that can be used in items such as clothing, cups, food containers, candy wrappers, and home and office furnishings, all as a whole new range of products. CDP now cooperates with international market leaders to develop products from the new PLA.

What these dynamics show is that portfolio building blocks may evolve into another form if the business environment demands this. Developments in the industry the firm is operating in and changes in its technology strategy determine the composition of the alliance portfolio (the mix of option, project and competence alliances) at one point in time, as well as the transformation of portfolio building blocks. By maintaining a portfolio of option, project and competence alliances firms thus enlarge their strategic possibilities.

Conclusion

High-tech firms operating in dynamic environments form alliances for knowledge acquisition that fit their technology and learning strategy. They can either exploit existing capabilities by linking up with firms in their own technology cluster or they can explore new combinations of knowledge in allying with partners from different technological clusters. Most firms choose for a combination of both learning strategies, in order to prevent technological inertia and undeveloped ideas. In order to realize the fit between technology strategy and the turbulence of the industry, firms have to build a portfolio of relationships. This portfolio can consist of three portfolio building blocks:

- option alliances, which aim at scanning the environment for new technologies;
- project alliances, which are intended to combine technological knowledge to develop a new technology or product through successive cooperation;
- core competence alliances, which aim at seeking complementary capabilities through cooperation, which are crucial to their core competence.

Firms that have created the right mix of building blocks in their alliance portfolio will be better able to meet the diverse demands of a high tech business environment.

Each portfolio building block can be a stepping stone to another building block. This transformation should be a consciously chosen path, depending on the composition of the alliance portfolio, given the firm's industry and technology strategy.

References

Brass, D.J., K.D. Butterfield and B.C. Skaggs, 1998, "Relationships and unethical behavior: A social network perspective", *Academy of Management Review*, 23(1), 14–31.

Burt, R.S. 1983, "Distinguishing relational contents", in R.S. Burt & M.J. Minor (Eds.), *Applied Network Analysis* (pp. 35–74), Beverly Hills, CA: Sage.

Duysters, G., A.D. Man and L. Wildeman 1999, "A Network Approach to Alliance Management", *European Management Journal*, 17(2).

Gomes-Casseres, B., 1996, *The Alliance Revolution: The New Shape of Business Rivalry*. Cambridge, Massachusetts: Harvard University Press.

Granovetter 1973, "The Strength of Weak Ties", *American Journal of Sociology*, 78(6).

Gulati, R., 1998, "Alliances and Networks", *Strategic Management Journal*, 19(4).

Spekman, R. and C.J. Lambe, 1997, "Fruit Fly Alliances", *The Alliance Analyst*, *1997* (August 15), 1–4.

Vasudevan, A. and G. Duysters 1998, "Towards an optimal portfolio of alliances and its impact on organizational performance", White paper, TUE, Eindhoven.

Chapter 11

Making Alliances Work: Lessons from the Airline Industry

Pieter Bouw

L14
L24
L93

In the airline industry, alliances have rapidly become key to attaining competitive advantage. The first major alliance was concluded between KLM and Northwest Airlines in 1989. Since then, a number of alliance groups have come into being. In the 1990s dozens of alliances have been concluded in the airline industry and the game is not over yet. In January 2000 three major alliance groups could be distinguished. The Wings alliance (consisting of KLM, Northwest, Continental and Alitalia) now competes with the Star Alliance and the OneWorld alliance (see Figure 1). A fourth group (Qualiflyer) is left without major partners,

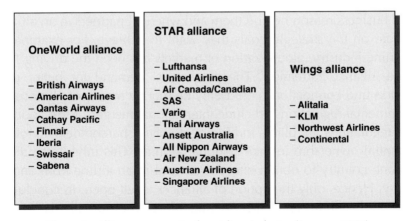

Figure 1. Alliance groups in the airline industry (January 2000).

when some of the members defected to the other alliance groups. Since January 2000, these constellations have continued to change. KLM for example has ended the partnership with Alitalia.

The large number of alliances in the airline industry by no means indicates that it is easy to form alliances. Quite to the contrary: making alliances work is an onerous task. In this article, a number of key lessons from practice are discussed, which together constitute an important part of the CEO's agenda for alliance management. The questions facing the CEO can be related to four consecutive phases of alliance management:

- establishing the reasons for partnering;
- getting to know your partner;
- concluding the alliance;
- managing implementation.

These four phases will now be discussed. In each phase, top management needs to pay attention to a variety of issues.

Be Clear About the Reasons for Partnering

In many sectors alliance activity is increasing. Clearly, alliances are in fashion. However, alliances will only be successful when there is a sound business reason behind them and when all partners in an alliance are clear on the strategic goals they want to achieve. For example, in the airline industry, globalization of markets has been the driving force behind alliance formation. The passengers' demand for better route networks and connections could only be met by means of alliances, as governmental regulations preclude international mergers. Most countries have regulations in place forbidding foreign shareholders to obtain substantial ownership in their national airlines. This inhibits an airline from one country to obtain effective control in an airline from another country. Hence, only the option of alliances is left open. In conclusion, in the airline industry clearly identifiable drivers for allying were at work, which made alliances both necessary and feasible.

The precise type of alliance is determined by two other characteristics of airlines. The first characteristic is that airlines have high fixed costs, while no inventory of finished products can be held. This means that the possibilities for optimization and realizing economies of scale increase dramatically, when firms cooperate intensively in a number of fields. Secondly, consumers are anonymous and replaceable. The only way for airlines to create loyal customers, is to offer better value (e.g. by extending the reach of loyalty programs) and better connections. These two features drive airlines towards alliances, which involve their entire business. This differs from other sectors in which alliances are normally limited to one part of a firm's business (for example R&D alliances or sourcing relationships). Other sectors in which alliances involve entire businesses are telecom, banking and energy/utilities. Unsurprisingly, the two characteristics of high fixed costs and anonymous customers are applicable to these sectors as well.

If the economic drivers in an industry lead firms to opt for alliances, they are well advised to think through what benefits they desire to gain. Three gains from partnering can be distinguished:

- economies of scale, which may derive from an increase in production;
- economies of scope, which may be reaped when several services or products can make use of the same production process;
- economies of skill, which emanate from complementary competencies and learning.

Partners need to have a clear view on the question, which of these economies are important in a specific alliance, especially because each of these economies requires a different type of management. Partners often focus on economies of scale and scope, while economies of skill are underestimated in importance. In the KLM–Northwest alliance however, economies of skill proved to be very interesting. The partners' knowledge and competencies were complementary, allowing each partner to learn from the other. This was not expected at the outset, but once it became clear that value could be created by exchanging knowledge, management processes were set up to increase this knowledge exchange. KLM was good at route planning and developing and managing hub and spoke systems. Northwest had built up a competence in financial engineering and yield and capacity management (deciding what the optimum mix of traffic is for a certain flight, e.g. the number of business class versus economy class passengers). Transferring this knowledge between the companies made a considerable contribution to the success of the alliance. For this aim, working groups were set up consisting of specialists in these fields from both partners. Because specialists have an innate drive to apply the best methods, transfer of skills took place rapidly and benefits were realized that went beyond the expected economies of scale. Although economies of skill may be hard to quantify, it does pay off to try to assess them before an alliance is concluded.

Get to Know Your Partner

When a firm has defined its goals for the alliance, it can enter the process of partner selection. In this phase, the key is to get to know your partner. Sufficient time must be dedicated to understand the partners' motives, goals and sincerity. When KLM was investigating the possibility of a partnership with SAS, Swissair and Austrian Airlines, quite some time was spent on these issues. After all, this was a very complex alliance, involving four airlines, seven governments and 21 unions. In such a complex environment, mutual understanding is a necessity for the alliance to work. What are the reasons for entering into a partnership and what are the major concerns when executing it? To obtain insight in the structural background for partnering, potential partners should discuss the next questions:

- What are your strong and weak points?
- What are your partner's strong and weak points?

In order to address cultural differences, you have to get a clear view on the norms and values of your partners. This can be realized by discussing the next two questions and analyzing them mutually:

- What do you think of your partners?
- What do you think your partners think of you?

Especially the last question can be very revealing, because the self-image of a firm can be quite different from the way in which its partners perceive it. By being aware of this early on, quite some problems can be avoided in the later phases of allying. Understanding the own and the partner's pitfalls and possibilities, smoothes the alliance process.

Getting to know your partner is even more relevant in the case of partnering with competitors. Three phases should be considered here. First, one has to trust the integrity of the partner. This trust is built over time by finding out why the partner wants to be involved in the partnership. Only when the partner's motives are sincere and (potential) win-win situations will prevail over win-lose or lose-lose, partners can move on to the next phase. The second phase is about showing vulnerability. In this phase, partners share data that the other partner can use in the competitive arena. The business case for the alliance is prepared at this stage. Because this requires cooperation between the organizations involved, this provides an excellent opportunity to measure the confidence employees of the separate organizations have in the partnership. Finally, partners have to agree not to use the information they have gathered about each other, in the competitive arena. It must be observed however, that facts and information are usually of less value to competitors than firms think. Besides, the speed of change in the market is so high nowadays, that "trade secrets" often loose value rapidly. Consequently, secrecy in alliances, though important, is less relevant than most firms think.

Conclude the Alliance

When a partner has been found, it is good to step back before concluding an alliance, to make sure that the alliance is not entered into in the "heat of the moment." A CEO should ask himself three questions, before definitely deciding to enter into an alliance:

1. Does it sound good?

Can the idea behind the partnership be easily explained? Only if a manager is able to explain the alliance logic in simple terms, he has a clear view on the value added of the alliance. Moreover, given the fact that communication is of prime importance in alliances, a clear story is a valuable thing to have. It simplifies communication towards employees, clients and shareholders. In short: it must be possible to explain the logic behind the alliance in a few words, taking not more than eight seconds in a TV-interview.

2. Does it add up?

The answer to this question comes from a thorough business analysis. Do both partners understand what it takes in terms of resources? What is the expected synergy? What are advantages and disadvantages of the partnership? Does the alliance match with the aims? If the aim is to reap economies of scale, overlap between partners indicates potential for improvement in particular regarding cost savings. If the aim of the alliance is to gain economies of scope, complementarity is important, as this will generate potential for revenue growth. In that case overlap between partners becomes less desirable. In case of economies of skill, stock must be taken of each other's competencies. All these issues need to be researched in detail.

3. Does it feel good?

Good personal relationships are a key to alliance success. Cultural complementarity is important as well. A good feeling about a partner in this regard is a *conditio sine qua non* for successful alliances.

If the answer to these three questions is positive, then the alliance can be concluded and the implementation challenge begins.

Managing Implementation

In the alliance literature most attention is paid to strategy, partner selection and forms of alliances. Literature on alliance implementation is relatively scarce, despite the fact that many interesting topics can be raised about this subject.

The first relevant topic is managing the differences between firms. As stated above, differences between firms complicate alliances. However, they also provide marvelous opportunities for learning from each other. If firms actively pursue taking over the strong points of their partner, they can reap quite some benefits. In the case of Northwest and KLM this is exactly what happened. Northwest for example had a predominantly short-term orientation, whereas KLM was inclined to look at the long-term. Both firms missed opportunities because of these focuses. In the alliance, both firms learned how to balance the short and the long-term views much better than before. Concluding: instead of blotting out differences, one should try to exploit them.

This is also true for cultural differences. Company cultures should not be mixed. Rather, partners should try to learn from each other's culture. Cultural differences are often intertwined with structural differences. For example, firms that have a functional structure, work quite differently from firms having a business unit structure. Across countries, differences in governance systems are determinants of company behavior. A one-tier structure is different from a two-tier structure. The long term view of KLM can partly be attributed to the two-tier structure, whereas the short term view of Northwest emanated from a more direct pressure of shareholders for higher earnings per share.

Other than in the case of mergers and acquisitions, such differences do not have to be eradicated. Whereas mergers and acquisitions require rapid integration of partners into one coherent firm, in alliances the emphasis should be on coordination between different partners. A common vision and building trust are more important for this than fast integration. One similarity between mergers, acquisitions and alliances is that both need to deliver visible results quickly, to uphold the drive in the implementation process.

A second underestimated aspect of alliances, is the impact they have in the internal organizations of the partners. This impact can have both a structural and an emotional component. An example of a structural component is that alliances often influence the budgets of business unit managers, without them being able to exert any control on that. If an alliance requires them to invest or make extra costs, while they are being held accountable for meeting their one-year budget target, they may become uncooperative. In that case it is the task of the CEO to change the accountability in his firm. As alliances hardly leave any aspect of business untouched, this can be a complicated and extensive task. But the accountability of the organization must match the accountability of the alliance.

Emotional aspects also require attention. Firms, which are used to act autonomously, at once become partly dependent on their partner. For many people this can be hard to accept. Fear for dependence of the organization can coincide with fear for the individual career. This may reduce commitment to the alliance and increase skepticism. In practice the best way to deal with this, is to appoint the best managers in important positions in the alliance. Employees can tell when the best man for the job is not appointed. This usually destroys commitment immediately. Appointing the best people is on the other hand a major commitment building act. In short: appoint those people you need somewhere else. Ultimately, the credibility of the management team determines the attitude of the rank-and-file vis-à-vis the alliance.

A third aspect of implementation is the preemption of problems. The first three months of a partnership are very rewarding. New ideas are being developed, new approaches identified. After that period, reality sets in and problems begin to appear. Things are not as easy as they appeared to be at first sight and the differences between the partners may lead to some irritation. It is in this phase that it becomes clear, whether the "Does it add up?" analysis was rightly executed. To prevent any problem from becoming a continuous source of irritation, conflicts need to be moved up the hierarchy at the right time. Escalation of conflicts can be avoided by means of structural and cultural approaches:

- Structural approach. In the Northwest–KLM alliance this was handled by a linking pin system, in which each working group contained a member who also was involved in a higher level-working group. In this way, problems were automatically brought up the hierarchy.
- Cultural approach. A culture which is forward looking and sees future opportunities, is better able to deal with current problems and tensions than a culture which is mainly oriented towards today. Appealing future gains make current problems seem less of an obstacle.

Hence, both the rational and the non-rational aspects must be addressed to avoid escalation of problems.

The CEO's Agenda

Making alliances work requires a continuous effort of CEO's in many fields and in different phases of the alliance process. Each phase has its own challenges and questions to answer. Figure 2 gives a brief overview of the key aspects of allying, as discussed above.

In alliances nothing goes automatically. Their impact on the organizations involved can be considerable. Any major alliance will take a substantial amount of management time. The practical lessons presented above will however contribute to a smoother and more efficient alliance process.

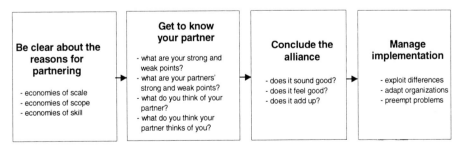

Figure 2. The CEO's agenda.

Pieter Bouw is the former CEO of KLM and has extensive experience in managing alliances. He currently holds a chair as a professor at the University of Twente.

Chapter 12

A Culture of Cooperation?
Not Yet

Arvind Parkhe

L14
L24
L93

Alliances are here to stay. Even the smartest, biggest, and richest companies have learned the value of competing through cooperation. With shortening product life cycles, rising cost pressures, and growing demands to respond to specific host government requirements and consumer tastes, companies seem to have accepted as fact the premise that remaining a corporate loner is simply not an attractive option. Observers of the business landscape note, with merit, how the current wave of alliances involves not just peripheral products, geographic markets, and technologies, but also those that touch the very core of alliance participants' vital competitive advantages. So alliances are fast becoming a mainstay of competitive strategy, rather than a transitional ploy helping corporate executives grope toward more permanent solutions. And because the underlying forces that have spawned alliances are mounting, not abating, alliances will continue to proliferate as well.

Take the global airline industry. Certainly this industry includes mega-carriers, especially from the United States and Europe. Yet not one of them is competing alone. Each major US carrier has established strategic links with non-US companies. Thus, Delta Airways is linked with Swissair, Sabena and Austrian; American Airways with British Airways, US Airways, JAL, and Qantas; Northwest with Continental, KLM, and Alitalia; and United Airways with Lufthansa, SAS, Air Canada, Thai Airways, Varig, South African Airways, Singapore Airlines,

Air New Zealand, and Ansett Australia. These global alliances, not individual airline companies, are battling it out on a worldwide playing field. Pushing this thought further, several interesting observations can be offered regarding the likely course of companies and alliances in the foreseeable future:

- Companies will become more alliance-sophisticated. As the motivations for entering into alliances continue to strengthen, the abilities to spot good partners, lock them in early, craft suitable alliance structures, and develop trustful relationships will become key. Recognizing this, companies will strive to develop or acquire these new abilities.
- Companies will invest greater resources in alliances. As companies appreciate the perils of not using a carefully considered alliance strategy, they will invest greater resources (management time, funds, compatible infrastructure) so as to proactively form and manage alliances in ways that reduce misunderstandings, increase trust, and improve performance.
- Executive staffing will be powerfully affected. A greater emphasis on alliances will translate into a new focus on nurturing appropriate talent, the special breed of managers who can comfortably shuttle across the alliance membrane explaining opposing viewpoints, while creating relationships and building an environment of trust. Already evident in its nascency, this trend will escalate as executives are increasingly appointed to newly created, senior-level positions to oversee companies' external relations. The portfolio of responsibilities of these executives will include scanning, screening, and selecting partners; structuring alliances; calibrating trust levels; monitoring information flows to protect family jewels; and handling corporate divorces.
- There will be growing appreciation of the soft aspects of collaboration. Formal contracts, while necessary, are not a substitute for informal understandings. Trust plays an important (often dominant) role in successful alliances, and managers often cite lack of trust as a key reason for failed alliances. In response, managers will look anew for ways in which they can develop and increase trust levels.

The phenomenal growth in alliances in recent years has led some futurists to predict a new, emerging culture of cooperation, one which consists of softening attitudes and warming relations between erstwhile competitors. I disagree. True, the present period marks the gradual passing of the familiar, centuries-old model of a single, independent, autonomous company. But an alternative model based on a culture of cooperation is, not rapidly filling the vacuum left by this passing. At least two real obstacles stand in the way. Both are related to challenges involving trust building: reluctance and speed. Managers typically are imbued with hierarchical, bureaucratic, or clan control within their own firms, and they will be unwilling and unable to cede control over key resources to others outside of their firm, especially if their company has only recently jumped on the alliance bandwagon. This unwillingness and inability diminish opportunities for trust formation, which is at the heart of alliance success. Moreover, today's frenetic business environment is hardly conducive to the slow, patient nurturing of relationships, which is the usual path to building trust. Our lack of management know-how for high-velocity trust development places additional hurdles in the emergence of a culture of cooperation.

These challenges offer a rich business opportunity. In the past, during periods of high turbulence, formal instruments (credentials or certificates such as a 5-star hotel designation or a CPA diploma) were issued by professional bodies, so that holders of these instruments could provide implicit guarantees of their trustworthiness and performance to any third parties, even those with whom no direct interactions had taken place earlier. In this fashion, rather than relying on direct contact or informal reputation, trust became a saleable product that was produced in response to the market for trust. There exists today a large, untapped market for trust in alliances. Thus, an entrepreneur might initiate a service company that performs several useful functions: it builds a databank on companies and continually updates this databank; acts as a matchmaker for prospective alliance partners; serves an auditing/verification role to ensure quality of data; and acts as a clearing house of information (see Figure 1).

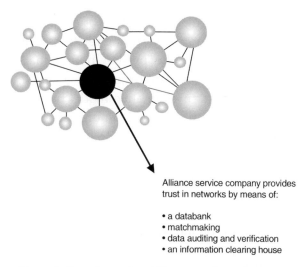

Alliance service company provides
trust in networks by means of:

• a databank
• matchmaking
• data auditing and verification
• an information clearing house

Figure 1. Functions of an alliance service company.

Today, even Corning Glass, one of the world's most successful practitioners of alliances, has to rely on third parties to learn how a potential partner conducts itself in an alliance. Information gathering is thus ad hoc and haphazard, since appropriate institutional mechanisms are not in place. It need not always remain so. Learning about a prospective alliance partner's trustworthiness remains as important today as in the past, but the tools used to obtain this knowledge must be adapted to the current high-velocity global environment. A service that offers reliable information to suit a company's geographic and strategic needs would fill this important niche. Such information might include, for example, a company's nationality and scope of worldwide operations, current resource availability, technical capabilities, past record of trustworthy behavior, and potential for cultural incompatibility. With such an institutional support system in place, the major obstacles to a true culture of cooperation will be removed, and it might even become possible to envision future alliance formation as straightforward as connecting components for a home audio and video system by different manufacturers.

Editors

Ard-Pieter de Man

Ard-Pieter de Man is Chief Executive Officer of the Centre for Global Corporate Positioning (CGCP, an Internet-based alliance knowledge centre) and an Associate Professor of Strategy at Maastricht University/ MERIT. He has worked as a fellow of the Nolan Norton Institute, the research branch of Nolan Norton & Co, part of KPMG Consulting. His work focuses on alliances and networks, especially in a new economy context. He is the (co-)author of some 20 articles and a number of books in this field, among which *Competing for Partners* (co-written with Han van der Zee and Daisy Geurts) dealing with the management of supplier relationships, alliances and networks. In 1999 he was the recipient of the ROA-award, handed out by the Dutch Council of Management Consultants, for his work in the field of alliance capability.

Geert Duysters

Geert Duysters (1966) is currently working as a Full Professor of Organization Science at the faculty of Technology Management of the Eindhoven University of Technology. He is acting as the Director of the Eindhoven Centre for Innovation Studies (ECIS). He holds an MBA degree from the University of Maastricht and a PhD in economics from the Maastricht Economic Research Institute on Innovation and Technology (MERIT). He worked as a part-time consultant (senior manager) for KPMG Alliances at the international headquarters in Amstelveen (the Netherlands) and is a board member of the Association of Strategic Alliance Professionals (ASAP). He also works as an alliance expert for the European Commission and the OECD and was one of the founders of the International Center for Alliances, Networks and Strategic Innovation (ICANSI). He currently serves as the Chairman of the supervisory board of the Centre for Global Corporate Positioning (CGCP, an Internet-based alliance knowledge centre). His main areas of interest are in international business strategies and strategic alliances. Professor Duysters published over 25 articles on alliances in international refereed journals and books.

Ash Vasudevan

Ash Vasudevan is a Managing Director of Strategic Alliances and CN Ventures at CommerceNet. He is also a founding partner of ICANSI and serves as its Chairman and CEO. He has a doctorate in International Business and Strategic Management, and is an expert in the areas of Alliances and networks, strategic innovation, e-commerce and internet strategy, technology and innovation management, competitive and change management. His primary interest is studying the intersection and interrelationship of business and technology with Internet, and its business, social, political and economic implications on a global basis. He has been featured speaker at many conferences on this topic. Aside from being an active strategy consultant for many Fortune 500 companies and the European Commission, he has also worked as Professor of Strategy and International Business at Washington State University and Director of Strategic Business Development and Alliance Practice for Alliance Management International. He also serves on the advisory board of ASAP Silicon Valley chapter, wildoscar.com, redmind.com, priceahead.com, eculture.com, cyberalliance.com, and the Brillianz Group.

Contributors

Sven Bakkes

Almost a year ago Sven, together with a close friend, founded The Brillianz Group. The company focuses on helping clients to transform their business models to effectively compete in the new economy. Core to Brillianz' philosophy is to work together intensively, with both client and partner organizations, to deliver complete eBusiness solutions. Before founding Brillianz, Sven was an active researcher at Eindhoven University of Technology, with special interests in strategic alliances, innovation management, and eBusiness. Sven has been involved in several research projects for well-known organizations such as KMPG Management Consultants, Philips Electronics NV, and Cap Gemini. Additionally, Sven holds an MBA degree from Maastricht University in International Business. He completed this study after a four-month stay in Santa Clara, Silicon Valley.

Bonnie Beerkens

Bonnie Beerkens (1975) studied International Business Studies at the University of Maastricht. After her graduation Bonnie started working as a tutor at the Faculty of Economics and Business Administration, at the University of Maastricht where she taught propaedeutic as well as graduate courses on international strategy and management. In 1999 she started her work as a PhD-student for ECIS (Eindhoven Centre for

Innovation Studies) at the Eindhoven University of *Technology, Faculty of Technology Management.* Bonnie's PhD thesis will aim at finding an optimal portfolio of strategic technology alliances for firms in turbulent industries. This topic will be embedded in a framework of social network theory, specifically alliance networks. Further social capital, organizational learning, technology life cycle and option theory are fields of interest for this study.

John Bell

John Bell is Corporate Alliance Manager at Philips Electronics. As such he is responsible for increasing the captured value potential by Philips in its alliances. The focus here is on institutionalizing alliance management and strengthening the alliance capabilities within Philips. Before he joined Philips, John was a Strategy Consultant at PricewaterhouseCoopers. In addition to being closely involved in many strategy development clientwork, he was responsible for the global Alliance Centre of Expertise. John started his career as Assistant Professor Strategic and International Management at Tilburg University. Here he wrote his PhD (with honor) on joint ventures and international expansion. John published extensively on strategic alliances in international and national journals and books.

Pieter Bouw

Pieter Bouw is the former CEO of KLM (the Royal Dutch Airlines) and has extensive experience in concluding and managing alliances. His most important accomplishment in this regard, has been the alliance between KLM and Northwest Airlines, covering the North Atlantic route. He currently holds a chair as a professor of management at the University of Twente.

Carlos García-Pont

Carlos García-Pont is an Industrial Engineer by the UPC (Spain). He has an MBA degree from IESE Business School and a PhD in International

Management from the Sloan School of Management (Massachusetts Institute of Technology). His research has been focused on two streams within the international management field, the development of alliance networks and the role of subsidiary strategy within multinational corporations. He has consulted on both with major companies. His writings have appeared in *Strategic Management Journal and European Management Journal* among others.

Daisy Geurts

Drs. T.W. (Daisy) Geurts is a research coordinator and consultant at the Nolan Norton Institute. She is responsible for the coordination of the activities of the Nolan Norton Institute. As a consultant, she participated in several projects in the information and communication industry. Her areas of expertise comprise alliances, networks and electronic commerce. Before joining the Nolan Norton Institute, she held a position at KPN Research, where she was involved in projects focusing on new business development, electronic commerce and new organizational forms.

Ben Gomes-Casseres

Ben Gomes-Casseres is an authority on corporate alliances and international business. He has researched these topics for ten years, taught them to MBAs and executives, and consulted with major companies in the United States and abroad. He is currently Associate Professor and Director of the MBAi Program at the Graduate School of International Economics and Finance, Brandeis University. His research, teaching, and consulting focus on alliance strategy and management, with an emphasis on high-technology fields. Ben holds the Bachelor of Arts degree from Brandeis, the masters in Public Affairs degree from Princeton University, and the Doctor of Business Administration degree from Harvard University.

Charmianne Lemmens

In 1999 Charmianne Lemmens started working as a PhD student for the Eindhoven Centre for Innovation Studies (ECIS) at the Eindhoven University of Technology at the Faculty of Technology Management at the Department of Organization Science. Her PhD thesis will address group-based competition in high technology industries and therefore she will conduct an empirical analysis of inter-alliance technological rivalry. Her research interests are in strategic alliances, alliance network formation, social network analysis, constellations, group-based competition and social capital.

Robert Porter Lynch

Robert Porter Lynch is CEO of The Warren Company, a dedicated alliance consultancy. Mr. Lynch is founding chairman of the Association of Strategic Alliance Professionals and holds a Master's degree in Organizational Development from Harvard University and a Bachelor's degree in International Relations from Brown University. He is a faculty member of the American Management Association, Canadian Management Centre. He has been involved in enhancing collaborative activity for scores of companies in a wide variety of industries. His clients have included a large number of Fortune 500 firms. He is the author of a number of award winning and best selling books on alliances. He is often quoted in business journals such a *Nations Business, The Wall Street Journal,* and *The Conference Board Reports.* Robert serves on the Board of Directors of several hi-tech companies.

Arvind Parkhe

Arvind Parkhe is an associate professor of International Business and Strategy at the Kelley School of Business, Indiana University, Bloomington. Following middle management experience with a German multinational firm in Germany and North America, he obtained a

PhD from Temple University. His research focuses on global strategic alliances and international joint ventures. In particular, he is interested in "soft" aspects of alliance management, including culturally based differences in trust and their impact on effective knowledge transfer. He currently serves on the editorial boards of the *Academy of Management Review, Journal of International Business Studies*, and *Journal of International Management.*

Larraine D. Segil

Larraine Segil is CEO of Larraine Segil Productions Inc, a virtual corporation whose products and services span the globe with partners in multiple channels (web-based programs, videos, satellite television, monthly columns, email newsletters, live executive education, speakers bureaus and keynotes, in person courses, audio books, books, software, comic strips, e-forums, consultancy). Larraine Segil Productions, Inc also distributes Segil's video series on Thought Leadership in E-Business, Alliances, E-Leadership and Global Management. She is also co-founder of The Lared Group, a Strategic Alliance Consulting Company.

Segil is the author of *FastAlliances™ for E-Business* (Wiley, pub date January 15, 2001) and *Intelligent Business Alliances* (Times Books, Random House) a bestseller according to the New York Review of Books. She presents senior executive programs on alliances for Caltech, Frost and Sullivan (UK and Germany), IMS (Scotland, Canada), Argentina, Chile, China, Singapore and throughout North America. Her web-based, Intranet, interactive program "Partnering for Results" is offered through the Ninth House Learning Network.

A regular commentator on CNN on alliances and mergers, Larraine has been featured in numerous magazines, including *Fast Company, Business Week, CFO, CIO* etc. She is a monthly correspondent for *IT Malaysia* and *IT Singapore.* She's a past columnist for *Industry Week Magazine*, and is on their panel of world experts who select the Top 100 companies annually. She speaks and consults worldwide on alliances. She is also the author of a novel, Belonging (available Amazon.com).

Phone: (310) 556-1778, fax (310) 556- 8085.
Website: www.lsegil.com and email: lsegil@lsegil.com.
Larraine Segil Productions Inc, 1801 Avenue of the Stars, Suite 505, Los Angeles, CA 90067, USA.

Ad van den Oord

Ad holds a Master degree in International Business from Maastricht University and a Bachelor degree in Building Economics and Property Development. He is specialized in ICT and International Strategy and Organization. After returning from a four-month stay in Silicon Valley, where he completed his MBA degree, Ad worked as an active researcher on eBusiness and eAlliances projects at Eindhoven University of Technology. Ad has been involved in research projects for KPMG Alliances, DSM, Origin, Cap Gemini, and the Dutch Ministry of Economic Affairs. Today, Ad is working full-time for his own company. The Brillianz Group, which he founded about a year ago, focuses on helping clients to transform their business models to effectively compete in the new economy. Core to Brillianz' philosophy is to work together closely, with both client and partner organizations, to deliver complete eBusiness solutions.

Joan E Van Aken

Joan E van Aken is Professor of Organization and Management at Eindhoven University of Technology, Faculty of Technology Management. His primary research interest concerns alliances and organizational networks, in particular in the field of product and process innovation. A second area of interest is research paradigms and methodologies and design theory.

He studied Applied Physics at Delft University of Technology and got his PhD in Business Administration at Eindhoven University of Technology. Prior to becoming a full professor he worked for some 20 years in industry, first in Operations Research and Logistics and subsequently as consultant, and as manager of consultants in the field of Strategy and Structure. Alliance formation and management was an important issue in his consultancy work.

He was for many years member of the Board of the OOA, the Dutch Institute for Management Consultants and is chairman of the Board of NOBO, the Dutch Organization for research in Business Administration.

Han van der Zee

Prof. Dr. Ing. J.T.M. (Han) van der Zee is the director of the Nolan Norton Institute, the research arm of Nolan, Norton & Co. He is responsible for Thought Leadership initiatives for business strategy, organizational renewal and IT strategy. He has provided extensive consulting services to senior business management in Europe and the US. He is also a professor of Business Transformation & IT at the Tilburg University in the Netherlands, and he is the author of several books and articles and speaks regularly at public conferences.